Succession for Change

Harry Korine

Succession for Change

Strategic transitions in family and founder-led businesses

Harry Korine
INSEAD
Fontainebleau, France

ISBN 978-3-319-52119-0   ISBN 978-3-319-52120-6   (eBook)
DOI 10.1007/978-3-319-52120-6

Library of Congress Control Number: 2017932891

Cover design by Samantha Johnson

Printed on acid-free paper

This Palgrave Macmillan imprint is published by Springer Nature
The registered company is Springer International Publishing AG
The registered company address is: Gewerbestrasse 11, 6330 Cham, Switzerland

Foreword

While the concept of Succession for Change sounds easy and certainly appeals to one's common sense, the deeper meaning of the idea and the practice are quite a different matter. Harry Korine's book is not professing to be a manual on how to achieve Succession for Change, rather it invites the reader to think profoundly about the subject, to get immersed in the concept and to then look around and analyze the ideas presented in light of their personal situation and experience. This is when one can start to ask oneself some rather weighty questions about the nature of succession. After all, as Harry points out, successions have been planned, with lesser or greater consequence, over millennia. It seems in fact, that since man could record these matters, we know about the results of successions that worked well and those that were abject failures. Most, if not all successions as Harry further states, have intended to preserve the legacy of the past, to honor that legacy and hence, as a consequence have limited change. There is not much argument that there were sound reasons in the past to prevent dramatic variances from the legacy laid down by forefathers or indeed business founders. Families were then, and today are, not keen to bet their entire business on risky adventures nor are they keen to follow the rash ideas of youth who may lack maturity and experience. However, as Harry suggests, perhaps these rules should be revisited. Is it possible or probable that the approach to preserving a family business must be reconsidered in light of the speed of change? Do families need to consider Succession FOR Change because by not doing so, they risk their entire enterprise and legacy?

When I think about the topic of Succession I am immediately drawn to the concept of legacy. One of the difficult conundrums of family business has always been the confluence of family and business. While numerous consultants are now vested in explaining the tension that exists as a result of that confluence and offering their services to help families legislate around the issues, few spend much time thinking about what is fundamental to the concept of legacy. If one were to ask tens of families to define the concept, one would receive as many definitions as questionnaires. It is certain that amongst those definitions there would be a fair mix of principle and artifact with concepts such as: everyone from the shop floor to the executive suite punches a time card; only the male line of the family can lead the business; our business is providing personalized transport for the masses, etc. However, are some of these not actually artifacts or definitions of what we DO today and what we DID yesterday? How do these types of statements help define what we should DO tomorrow? Is it possible by the time family constitutions have been written, visions conceived and the half a dozen other steps taken as prescribed as necessary for the preservation and the continuity of the family business, that all the forces internally that might have encouraged change have been effectively tamped down? The process itself of formulating and agreeing, as a family, on any statements of intent, visions, and constitutions, requires collaboration and consensus. These are processes that are contrarian to facilitating change. This naturally leads to the questions of how to allow change to happen while "preserving the legacy".

What if the focus of the legacy discussions was changed from preservation to *honoring* instead? Does the process of agreeing what that honor should be allow the family to regard that which made them, their founders and their businesses great while freeing them from the shackles of continuing to do that which they always did? If principles or ways of conducting business are honored does this then permit one to be more strategic in the analysis of those businesses? As Harry asks, are the advantages of "patient capital" and the resulting large investments in capital structures, hallmarks of family businesses, still the competitive advantages they once were? In fact, have these large investments become the albatross of family business because they hold back the already conservative natures of family business from moving away from the legacy businesses? So if family businesses could separate the discussion around what to honor and hence, preserve, from the discussion of business strategy, would this allow succession for change? If a family were able to identify the true "golden goose" in the business as opposed to legacy endeavors which had their moment but which are either no longer competitive or even relevant, what would that bring? Defining what the "golden goose" is takes fortitude and courage. It may be what made the company great is no longer relevant and is being held on to as a relic for the sake of "legacy" or to honor the dead or the older generation. What is paying the bills is what matters. What also matters is to consider freeing up unproductive assets and deploying them systematically in carefully selected bets so as to ensure that there will be a new "golden goose" in the future. This might be coupled with a shared family understanding around true risk. That is, the risk of not changing is greater than the risk of change. Changing does not mean betting the whole business. It does mean thinking about securing that part of the business that is earning its keep while taking calculated risks with the capital that is not.

In summary, Harry's thoughtful and provocative book—Succession for Change invites all business families to consider what is being risked by changing versus trying to preserve a legacy that might inhibit the change that will allow them to successfully move into the next generation.

Senior Vice President & Head of Corporate Development,   Valerie A. Mars
Mars Incorporated
Non-Executive Director, Fiat Chrysler Automobiles
Munich, Germany

Preface

Succession is the original governance challenge. The Bible, for example, describes how King David abdicated so that Solomon could succeed him and continue his work. In a different era, Genghis Khan put in place the key elements of a succession plan that would allow the consolidation of the Mongol empire he had founded. Other historical leaders, such as Alexander the Great or William the Conqueror, did not resolve their succession during their lifetime, bequeathing years of war to their would-be heirs. Rich in potential for conflict and essential to the human experience, succession has provided the raw material for well-known myths and famous works of literature. It is an age-old problem, but succession does not get old—leaders of every generation face it anew.

Is succession *manageable*? In "King Lear", in "Macbeth", and in "Hamlet", Shakespeare portrays rulers that fail in their attempts to shape the future beyond their own lifetimes. On the other hand, family businesses that thrive for decades and even centuries offer evidence of leaders who *are* able to prepare their organizations for succession. Under certain circumstances and with the proper steps, succession can succeed. As a body of knowledge has grown around the topic, a veritable industry of succession services has arisen to systematize the process of succession—consultants, lawyers, bankers, and personal advisors. With the professional help available today, Shakespeare's tragedies might have played out quite differently.

If the question of whether succession can be managed has been answered, why write about it now? In business, as in other walks of life, succession has traditionally focused on ensuring *continuity*. Today, with innovative challenges threatening established positions everywhere, succession has to establish a basis for *change*. The impermanence of competitive advantage fundamentally alters the rationale of succession in business—from ensuring continuity to enabling change. This shift affects all firms, but it is particularly troubling for family and founder-led businesses, where the shaping influence of family or founder can make it especially difficult for successors to transform the business. In family businesses that have been built over several generations, succession for change is up against loyalty to what the firm stands for; in first generation businesses, succession for change struggles with undoing the founder's own achievements.[1]

We know how to set up the institutions of leadership that support organizational continuity in family and founder-led businesses, but we do not know how to institutionalize succession for change. Unlike succession for continuity, succession for change is never just about a person; it involves questions of strategy, affects the balance of power in the firm and ultimately represents an entrepreneurial choice of what to do with the business.

Synopsis and Contribution

The book begins with an examination of the importance of the shaping influence of family or founder and articulates how a generalized concern over legacy sways both the theory and the practice of succession towards continuity. The second part of the book presents an analysis of how competitive advantage has evolved over the last twenty-five years and examines the approaches being adopted by current business leaders, succession service providers and the next generation to address the change imperative in succession. The concluding chapters assess the futures of family and founder-led businesses, present a framework for implementing succession as transformation, and rethink succession governance. I show that when change becomes the focus of succession, developing entrepreneurial values takes precedence over preserving the status quo; succession planning evolves from an episodic to a continuous process; and the emphasis of succession governance shifts from executive selection to strategic direction.

In reframing the age-old question of succession as an issue of entrepreneurial choice, the book breaks new ground. Concentrating on the vital challenge of succession for change and juxtaposing succession for change with the traditional focus on succession for continuity, I address a critical test for family and founder-led businesses and open up the field of succession planning to a rethinking of its tenets. In tackling the subject from theoretical and practical

---

[1] Approximately half of all family businesses can be classified as first generation. Astrachan, JH (2003) Commentary, Journal of Business Venturing, 18, 567–572.

angles, with consideration of the perspectives of current business leaders, advisors, and the next generation, I also depart from traditional research approaches. Most of the literature in the field works from a single angle and presents only one perspective. By embedding the question of succession in the full range of its interpretations, I am able to shed new light on a process that concerns many different actors.

Zurich, Switzerland   Harry Korine

Contents

Part I   Succession for Continuity   1

1   Succession to Preserve a Legacy   3

2   Continuity as an Outcome of Doing It by the Book   15

Part II   Succession for Change   25

3   The Change Imperative ... for Family and
    Founder-Led Businesses   27

4   Succession for Change in Current Practice   37

5   The World of Succession Services   51

6   Next Generation   63

Part III   Perspectives   75

7   Succession in a World of Change   77

8   Succession as Transformation   93

9   Rethinking Succession Governance   105

Epilogue. Succession—The Most Human
of Governance Challenges   117

Index   119

Author Bio

Harry Korine (PhD, INSEAD) teaches strategy at INSEAD and corporate governance at the London Business School, as well as the Hochschule St. Gallen. His research has resulted in several books and numerous articles, including "The Leap to Globalization" (Jossey-Bass, 2002), "Entrepreneurs and Democracy", (Cambridge University Press, 2008) and "When You Shouldn't Go Global", (Harvard Business Review, 2008). His most recent book, "Strong Managers, Strong Owners" (Cambridge University Press, 2014), explored the relationship between corporate governance and strategy. As a private consultant, he has advised family and founder-led businesses around the world on questions of strategy, governance, and succession.

List of Figures

Fig. 2.1   Doing it by the book: a complex process for continuity   24
Fig. 3.1   The impermanence of competitive advantage: change at every level   36
Fig. 4.1   Opposite extremes of succession: from divestment to return   50
Fig. 5.1   The evolution of succession services   60
Fig. 6.1   The next generation: from closed and isolated to open and linked   72
Fig. 7.1   The succession process: episodic vs. continuous   91
Fig. 8.1   Succession, strategy, and stakeholders   102
Fig. 9.1   Roles in succession governance   115

List of Tables

Table 7.1 Succession today: what is different? What is the same?   79
Table 9.1 Leadership involvement in the succession process: do's & don'ts   109

Part I

Succession for Continuity

I begin with an examination of the importance of the shaping influence of family or founder and articulate how a generalized concern over legacy sways both the theory and the practice of succession towards continuity. This provides the basis for understanding the magnitude of the shift represented by succession for change.

1

Succession to Preserve a Legacy

Legacy. Succession may remove the leader, but not the way of doing things—at succession, a legacy of policies and norms is often formally enshrined, even if it no longer suits the competitive context and reduces the effectiveness of the organization.

Psychology. Fear of mortality, development of trust, and loss of identity are psychologically profound challenges to both the departing leader and the organization left behind that are eased by the assurance of continuity.

Cultural History. From political history, we take the need for prudent choice; from religious history, the importance of the mantle of the founder; and from business history, the convention of generation spanning ownership defending a lasting legacy.

In this chapter, we examine the importance of the shaping influence of family or founder and articulate how a generalized concern over legacy sways thinking about succession towards continuity. The starting point for our observations is that successful organizations often outlive their leaders. If the imprint of the family or the founder is strong enough, however, policies and norms can persist, orienting decisions according to the formula established by the leader. In other words, succession may remove the person, but not his or her way of doing things—a legacy may remain, even if it no longer suits the competitive context and reduces the effectiveness of the organization.

We draw on individual and organizational psychology to show that preserving a legacy is of importance to both the departing leader and the succeeding generation. For the departing leader, succession means a loss of power and a confrontation with personal mortality. Between the leader and the successor, a concrete transmission of power takes place, a process that requires time and

© The Author(s) 2017
H. Korine, *Succession for Change*, DOI 10.1007/978-3-319-52120-6_1

trust. For the leader and the organization, finally, succession can imply a loss of identity and direction. Fear of mortality, development of trust, and loss of identity are psychologically profound challenges that are eased by the assurance of continuity in the trajectory of decisions as well as in the way of doing things.[1] Succession for continuity satisfies a generalized concern over legacy.

Passing the baton from one generation to the next is a quintessentially human process, and accumulated wisdom from the human past continues to color how we think about succession today. From political history, we take the need for prudent choice; from religious history, we refer to the notion of the mantle of the founder; and from business history, we note the convention of generation spanning ownership. Again, preserving a legacy is a critical consideration, for both the departing leader and the succeeding generation, and succession for continuity is the solution that best fits experience. In their predisposition to continuity, succession models in place today do not differ fundamentally from their counterparts in history.

1.1   From Influence to Legacy

Early on in the process of doing research for this book, I met with a wizened serial entrepreneur, a man who had founded more than half a dozen companies, some extremely successful, some only moderately so, and some not successful at all. Once he moved on from a company he had founded, he told me, he did not care anymore about what the company did or how it was run. Of course, he still cared about the people, as individuals, he remarked, but he was not at all concerned about his legacy at the company. In light of my experience with so many family and founder-led businesses where legacy matters very much, the serial entrepreneur's comments at first struck me as odd and even dangerous. How could he not care about his legacy? Since that meeting, I have had the chance to talk to a number of other serial entrepreneurs, and, by and large, they also didn't worry about whether the companies they had founded maintained *their* policies and norms. What a contrast to the founders and families who want the businesses they have shaped to remain in the family. For them, unlike for the serial entrepreneurs, leaving a legacy is very important, and succession typically triggers discussion about what the legacy should be and how it can be maintained. Particularly for the founder, but in practice also for the next generations of a firm that stays in the same hands, succession at the top is the crucible for considering the legacy that is to be passed on.

---

[1] For a summary, see Kets de Vries MFR (1985) The Dark Side of Entrepreneurship. Harvard Business Review 63, 160–167.

To anyone who has ever worked in a family or founder-led business, the shaping influence of family and/or founder is obvious and tangible. It affects both the content and the process of life in the firm, running the gamut from the seemingly inconsequential to the patently critical. Thus, at the one end, there might be influence over what associates wear and, at the other end, influence over what strategies are considered. Importantly, the shaping influence of family and/or founder extends to how decisions are made, based on what criteria and over what time frame. In many cases, the shaping influence is so strong that it does need to be spelled out—everyone knows what the family or the founder would do and how they would go about it. Beyond a certain point, growth of the business may necessitate a codification of policies and norms, but it is often only at the time of succession that leaders think of what needs to be preserved—once they are no longer there to ensure in person that their influence is heeded. This is when leaders still in place start to think about their legacy.

In family and founder-led businesses, succession raises the question of what comes after. On the one hand, there are legal and financial issues to address, to ensure that, as individuals, family members and founder are well taken care of. On the other hand, and of more direct relevance to this book, there are strategy and governance issues to deal with, to ensure that the firm has the right basis to carry on. Not infrequently, this latter concern leads to the formal articulation of what the firms stands for and what values will guide it going forward. Here we have the basis for the mission statements and value statements that are intended to solidify if not cement the policies and norms of the leaders in place. These statements are generally formulated in language that is global and non-specific: ownership constraint (who can own shares in the firm), business competence assurance (what kinds of areas the firm can enter into), decision-making process (how key decisions are made), etc. Nonetheless, taken as a basis of what the family or the founder wishes to be their legacy, these statements have a profound effect on the succession and on the business. This is the proverbial "hand from the grave" cast in writing. Since the overriding concern of legacy is preservation of what has been achieved and the future cannot be known, formal declarations of this type tilt the firm towards continuity.

Continuity is not always bad; on the contrary, continuity has always been one of the great strengths of family and founder-led businesses that survive for multiple generations. Often, respect for the legacy and steadfastness in the face of volatility have kept these kinds of firms out the expensive and potentially ruinous back and forth of economic cycles and managerial fashions. However, a concern with legacy tends to bias decisions towards continuity, even when continuity is inadequate for addressing the challenges faced by the firm. Thus, a statement of policies and norms that limits ownership flexibility, prevents the firm from going into new areas, and posits consensual decision-making may make it impossible or very difficult for the firm to respond to competitive challenges coming from deep pocketed new players from outside the industry. In other words, a concern with legacy may keep the firm stuck in its ways just when it most needs to adapt to changed market conditions. Again, succession serves as a catalyst for raising these questions, because it both triggers thinking about legacy and represents a real opportunity for change.

> <u>Going Against the Conventional Wisdom</u> :
> *An effective leader does not need to articulate and formalize a legacy.—*
> *As concerned as departing leaders generally are about their legacy, quite a few are hesitant or simply unwilling to undertake the effort required to articulate and formalize what their legacy is about. For some, their involvement in day-to-day affairs—until the last day—precludes them from doing any of the kind of reflective work necessary to capture their legacy in writing; for others, their sense of practicality recoils undertaking a structured legacy exercise. If only they work hard enough and forcefully instill their sense of values, so they reason, their legacy will live.*
> *The reality is that stories and examples do live on, but policies and norms have a shorter half-life. Once the leader moves on, he or she will continue to be referred to, but without a formal statement, signed and blessed by the family or the founder, successors are likely to disagree on significant points of both content and process and may even come into conflict. If the original leader is still around to be consulted, he or she may be called upon to take sides; if not and sometimes even if so, disagreements of this kind can lead to governance challenges and major disruptions in the life of the organization.*
> *For these reasons and even if they know that the so-called "hand from the grave" can undermine the functioning of the organization and limit its adaptability, many people at the top of family and founder-led businesses choose to formalize their legacy in the shape of mission and vision statements, sometimes also complemented by value statements. Formalizations like these are supposed to prevent conflict for generations to come. The irony, of course, is that in preventing conflict, they may also get in the way of necessary change.*

Why is legacy such an important consideration to the leader contemplating succession? In the following pages, we will examine two sources of the legacy focus: psychology and cultural history. Succession is never only about finding a new leader; it is always also about addressing the concerns of the departing leader. No matter the situation, whether the business is in outstanding health or in poor condition, the departing leader has to come to terms with his or her departure. Inevitably, this raises personal questions of mortality and loss that psychology can help explain. In view of the fact that succession is an age-old human question, the psychology of succession in turn cannot be fully understood without a deeper grounding in the cultural history of succession.

Both the psychology and the cultural history of succession suggest that a focus on legacy and the resulting preference for formalizing existing policies and norms make the process of succession easier for the departing leader and help the organization carry on. In other words, the concern for legacy makes it more likely that succession will be for continuity rather than for change.

1.2 Psychology and Cultural History

Psychology plays an important role in the management of succession, at several levels of analysis: that of the leader as an individual, that of the relationship between the leader and the successor, and that of the shared identity of the leader and the organization. For the leader as an individual, succession means a loss of power and, especially for the retiring leader, a confrontation with personal mortality. Between the leader and the successor, a concrete transmission of power takes place, a process that requires time and trust. For the leader and the organization, finally, succession can imply a loss of identity and direction. Fear of mortality, development of trust, and loss of identity are psychologically profound challenges that are eased by the assurance of continuity. Succession for change, on the other hand, compounds these challenges.

At the individual level, letting go can be very difficult. The cases in which leaders delayed succession in order to avoid letting go of power and preserve the illusion of immortality are too numerous to mention. Successful organizations, however, outlive their founders; they even outlive the leaders who succeed the founders. Recognizing this disparity and in cognizance of their own mortality, leaders often spend the final years of their reign focusing on their personal legacy. The focus on legacy can lead to multiple actions: putting in place contracts that determine the governance of the organization for years to come; making long-term, difficult to unwind investments that cement the leader's strategy choices; and choosing people who will maintain the culture built by the leader. On the surface, every one of these steps can be justified as contributing to the strengthening the organization. However, commitments to the legacy of the leader who cannot see beyond his/her time also contribute to rigidifying the organization, establishing boundaries that support succession for continuity and set further hurdles for change. Of course, warning voices will be heard, but the stronger the leader and the greater his/her impact on the organization, the more difficult it will be to argue against doing everything to perpetuate the leader's vision.[2]

---

[2] Cf. Sonnenfeld J (1988) The Hero's Farewell. Oxford University Press, New York.

The fear of mortality and the desire to leave a legacy also directly impact the choice of successor. A person with the same views as the leader is more likely to preserve and build on the leader's accomplishments. It follows that a person with the same views will have a higher probability of being chosen to succeed the leader. Add to the importance of legacy the importance of getting along with the leader and the leader's team in order to merit their confidence and trust, and it becomes clear why succession for continuity is the psychologically motivated default option for many decision makers. If not a relative or a friend, then at least a known quantity, vetted by years of experience and therefore predictable in his/her behaviors, represents a safer bet and is therefore a more legitimate recipient of the mantle of leadership than a candidate who stands for change. Again, warning voices may be heard, particularly from outsiders, such as advisors and independent directors, but outsiders are rarely trusted enough to fundamentally alter the course of as critical a decision as succession.

Organizations identify particularly strongly with their founders and with leaders who have had a profound impact. The succession of this kind of leader is seen as especially difficult, representing a major departure.[3] In many cases in fact, the imprint of the founder or of the influential leader is strong enough to persist, as the organization continues on a kind of autopilot, orienting decisions according the formula for success established by the departed leader. In other words, succession removes the person behind the formula for success, but the formula itself remains. Even if a change minded successor manages to get beyond the barriers of investment inertia and insider decision-making, he/she still has to face the routines and recipes identified with the past leader and ingrained in the organization. Again, this problem is much more pronounced in organizations with a history of success under the same leadership, such as family and founder-led businesses.

Going Against the Conventional Wisdom :
*   For the departing leader, succession is always a struggle.—*
*   There are numerous examples in family and founder-led businesses of the person at the top holding on to power for a long time, for too long in the eyes of neutral observers and way past retirement age. This holding on for too long is often a source of frustration for the next generation, as they spend years and years in a holding pattern— without substantial responsibility for the business and unfulfilled, but too committed to leave, playing Prince Charles to the leader's Queen Elizabeth. Although this is a common state of affairs and has its roots in the psychology of the successful leader, it doesn't have to be that way. For some leaders, succession is easy: (a) because they have a clear idea of what they want to do outside of the business after leaving; and (b) because they have confidence in a successor, selected and tested over a long period.*

---

[3] cf. Levinson H (1971). Conflicts That Plague the Family Business. Harvard Business Review 49, 90–98; Lansberg I (1988). The Succession Conspiracy. Family Business Review, 1, 2.

It is important not to wait for too long to start the process that prepares the leader for the next stage of his or her life and the business for the next stage of its existence. A leader who is already "overdue" is much harder to wean from the business than a leader who has started to think about separation when there was still time left for another life. There are no hard and fast rules for when is the right time, but beginning the discussion early makes it more likely that succession takes place smoothly, as the departing leader and the organization have all the time required to get ready. It is not true that nobody likes to talk about their own succession, but it is true that talking about succession takes courage, both on the part of the departing leader and on the part of the person or people bringing up the topic. This is courage in governance, as opposed to courage in business, and leaders of family and founder-led businesses should look for this kind of courage in the people they select to serve on their boards.

Succession doesn't have to be a struggle—the person at the top of a family or family-led business doesn't have to stay on for too long. Many will stay on for too long, and not many will prepare to step down of their own accord, but most would be grateful if a timely departure could be arranged. It is up to board members and trusted advisors to help leaders see their way to an exit that is both personally satisfying and good for the business.

The academic discipline of psychology only came into existence some one hundred years ago. The cultural history of European civilization, on the other hand, holds many centuries of lessons for succession in family and founder-led businesses. The biblical story of how King David chose Salomon to be his successor, how he passed over his older sons to enthrone the one who was dedicated to continuing his father's vision of nation-building and how he fought a war to silence the opposition of the rest of the family, contains the basic elements of a plan that modern day succession advisors would recognize: (a) choose a successor before you become incapacitated; (b) make the choice based on the qualities demonstrated by the person; (c) set up structures to ensure that the successor will carry on your work; and (d) be prepared to enforce your choice against opposition.[4] King David knew what he wanted the future to look like, and he also knew that his older son, Absalom, had a very different view. To prevent change, then, King David took the unconventional steps of disregarding the order of birth and abdicating in favor of Salomon. As history unfolded, these steps ensured continuity and allowed King David's vision to blossom, making for a model case of managing succession for continuity.

By contrast, historical cases of succession for *change* always seem to end in violence and upheaval—far from the ideal of a smooth transition of power. The death of Alexander the Great was followed by almost fifty years' of war

---

[4] The story of the succession of King David is based on the biblical account, 1 Samuel 16 to 1 Kings 2.

among the Diadochi (potential successors), dividing the erstwhile empire into many different kingdoms. Successions that are accompanied by attempts at regime change in "King Lear", "Macbeth", and "Hamlet" all end in war, with the original protagonists killed and political outcomes uncertain. In the celebrated dictum of Louis XV of France, finally, the king himself appears to predict that succession in the context of change must lead to disaster, when he says "après moi le déluge". Archetypical examples like that of King David provide leaders with clear points of reference for managing succession for continuity that are echoed in modern practice; succession for change, on the other hand, belongs to a different category of historical events—harder to predict and much more difficult to influence in the desired direction.

The story of King David represents a case of managed succession for continuity under monarchy. Like monarchs, the emperors of old had absolute power; unlike monarchs, they rarely built family dynasties. In the Roman Empire, for example, emperors chose their successor, but not necessarily or even most commonly from their own family. Instead, Roman emperors followed the lines of King David in choosing a successor who was capable, would loyally continue their work, and could count on the necessary support of the Senate. Even though it often worked as intended, this model of succession also bore the potential for conflict, and many successions were marked by dispute and resort to arms (for example, the succession of Julius Caesar). However, the extent and the duration of the Roman Empire helped anchor the idea of *actively choosing* a successor for continuity in European political culture.

In religion, the question of succession is intimately tied to the idea of carrying the mantle of the prophet, the person who communicated directly with God.[5] The mantle of the prophet is what legitimizes successors to lead the people and pronounce on matters of dogma, and this is why successors lay a claim to it. Having been chosen by the prophet or having been with the prophet allows successors to speak with his authority, against all those with different views who cannot assert such a tie. This is a very important idea in the study of succession and is echoed in business succession, where a personal connection with the founder lends credibility to leadership and is therefore an important criterion for choosing successors. Like in religion, the transmission of power in business may be accompanied by a ritual touch that ties generations of successors to the founder—a figurative sword on the shoulder. A personal connection with the founder gives the successor a part of the founder's air of sanctity.

---

[5] The idea derives from the story of passing of Elijah's mantle in 2 Kings 2 and has become part of clerical practice in Judaism, Christianity, and Islam.

The idea of carrying the mantle of the prophet goes hand in hand with the notion of establishing continuity as the primary purpose of succession. Succession in the history of religions is about continuing the work of the prophet and maintaining the dogma. The focus on continuity in religious succession has undoubtedly also had a normative effect in society: continuity is to be aspired to, and change is to be distrusted. Of course, succession in religion can make reference to change: Pope Francis I may have been chosen by the College of Cardinals at least in part to reform the inner workings of the Catholic Church, as John Paul II before him may have been chosen to help the Church face the political pressures of a changing world. However, fundamental change in the nature of religions does not come from succession. Rather, a new voice from the outside is needed, a new prophet in other words, who offers his own vision and then passes on *his* mantle to *his* successors. In this sense, also, religious history reinforces the general primacy of succession for continuity; it offers little insight on the process of managing succession for change.

Going Against the Conventional Wisdom :
Business leaders don't care about history.—
Whereas political leaders frequently make reference to historical figures, business leaders are much less likely to invoke this kind of history directly. Of course, they know the history of their industry and are clear on what has worked in the past and what hasn't. Thus, references to historical success formulae (i.e. going for market share in a new category) and historical errors (i.e. not letting foreign competition attack the home market) are common, but references to historical leaders are not. In part, this is because it is the ethos of modern business to always be at the forefront of technological and economic change, and references to historical figures in politics or business would clash with that ethos; in part, this is also because business leaders rightly hesitate to compare themselves with historical leaders, particularly those who have amassed a lot of power. And yet, business leaders generally do care very much about who and what comes after them, and, on this question, cultural history has a lot to offer.
Depending on where they are from and what kind of schooling they have had, business leader will have different stories and archetypes in the back of their minds when they are considering succession. In Judeo-Christian settings, the succession of King David casts a long shadow, while in Islamic settings, the succession of Mohammed is essential to understanding people and attitudes; in English speaking countries, the discouraging tale of King Lear is never far from the surface, while in China, the disastrous succession intrigue that led to the downfall of the Qin dynasty is well-known. In daily affairs, these stories are irrelevant, but with age and when the time comes to think about succession, they reemerge, as mileposts or as deterrents. They may or may not be explicitly referred to, but they are alive in the minds of leaders and the people around them.

Business may have little to do with history, but succession is about history, particularly so in family and founder-led businesses. For the departing leader more than anybody else, history can loom very large, as he or she fades into the organization's past. Not surprisingly, the departing leader would rather be remembered for leaving behind an organization that is intact and united behind the successor, than an organization that is unstable and internally split. Better to be remembered as a King David than as a King Lear.

The history of commerce is as old as that of human civilization, but for most of this history, the domain of commerce was narrowly defined, and the rules of succession were clear-cut. It was only in the eighteenth century that the corporation gained a separate legal status, allowing it to outlive its owner(s), and making it necessary to address the question of succession in a more nuanced way.[6] Family businesses had an eye on competence and loyalty as important considerations in the management of succession from early on. With the twin purposes of keeping the business healthy and keeping the business in the family, succession was managed to ensure continuity of development and continuity of ownership.[7]

1.3 Conclusion

The prospect of succession in family and founder-led businesses often goes hand in hand with concern about establishing a legacy. By establishing a legacy, often in the shape of formal vision and mission statements, a departing leader can ensure that the policies and norms that he or she stood for are maintained even after stepping down. Concern about leaving a legacy makes succession for continuity more likely than succession for change, because whereas continuity supports a legacy, change can threaten it. The departing leader's desire to leave a legacy and thereby ensure continuity finds its sources in individual psychology and in cultural history. Both psychology and the Western cultural history within it is embedded come down on the side of continuity, as a means of supporting the ability of the departing leader to leave in confidence and the organization to carry on effectively. Succession for change, by contrast, bears much more potential for conflict and failure.

---

[6] Gomez P-Y, Korine H (2008) Entrepreneurs and Democracy: A Political Theory of Corporate Governance. Cambridge University Press, Cambridge, UK.

[7] For further historical background on family businesses, see James H (2006) Family Capitalism: Wendels, Haniels, Falcks and the Continental European Model. Cambridge University Press, Cambridge, MA, and Payne P (1974) Industrial entrepreneurship and Management in Great Britain. In: Mathias P, Postan M (eds) The Cambridge Economic History of Europe. Cambridge University Press, Cambridge, UK, Volume 7; part 1; p 180–230.

Individual and organizational psychology offer persuasive arguments in favor of a legacy that enshrines continuity and makes change difficult. The departing leader will feel better about leaving, the successor will have an easier entry, and the organization will act with more confidence if succession is for continuity. The cultural history within which this psychology is embedded further supports the power of legacy and praises succession for continuity. From the Bible and political history, we take the necessity of prudent choice; from religious history, we derive the importance of carrying the mantle of the founder; in business history, we observe the convention of generation spanning (family) ownership defending the legacy of founder and family; and, by the classic tales of succession in literature, we are reminded of the human drama that accompanies succession for change. All of these ideas still have a place in the contemporary discussion of succession in family and founder-led businesses, and like the stories of King David and Alexander the Great continue to color our views of what succession should or should not look like, favoring succession for continuity and pointing out the difficulties of succession for change.

2

Continuity as an Outcome of Doing It by the Book

Succession Research. Research in succession builds on principles of psychology and leadership. Central normative insights are two: succession should be thought of as a process, rather than as an event; both the process and the outcome of succession should be tailored to fit the organization and the context.

Best Practice. A seriously considered succession process takes a significant amount of leadership time, requires the input of a variety of voices and involves more than just the selection of a successor. Best practice in succession planning tilts the outcome of the process towards continuity.

Succession Services. An important part of doing succession by the book and following best practice is to engage the best advisors that money can buy and spending a lot of leadership time with them. Because continuity increases the likelihood of more business, advisors, too, tend to prefer continuity in succession.

Two principal normative insights emerge from research on succession in business: first of all, succession should be thought of as a process that unfolds over time, rather than as an event; second, both the process and the outcome of succession need to be tailored to fit the organization and its environment.[1] Treating succession as a process reinforces the tendency to favor continuity over change.[2] A process that takes time and, of necessity, involves many different contributors, is less likely to result in transformative change than a

---

[1] The literature on succession planning in family business is vast. For a particularly comprehensive review, see Handler WC (1994) Succession in family business: A review of the research. Family Business Review 7, 133–157.

[2] Lecouvie K, Pendergast J (2014) Family Business Succession: Your Roadmap to Continuity. Palgrave Macmillan, London. These recent authors make continuity the cornerstone of their argument.

© The Author(s) 2017
H. Korine, *Succession for Change*, DOI 10.1007/978-3-319-52120-6_2

snap decision. Of course, the process can be (and is often) designed to explicitly consider change, but length and depth reduce the chance of decision makers agreeing on a radical departure.[3]

As a process, the best practice of succession involves far more than just choosing a successor and handing over the reins—potential successors have to be identified and groomed; legacy, business, and governance questions, as well as legal and tax considerations have to be addressed; and the organization has to be prepared. Done well and with proper care, succession is a process that requires time and effort and cannot be delegated; it is one of the most important jobs of the leader and the principal decision makers in the business. Adapting the process and outcome of succession to the context means that each succession has to be customized, with necessary attention to the particularities of the situation. One size does not fit all, but there is a method for every situation, and many steps have been codified, onerous to go through but well established. As a general rule, complexity and structure in the process strengthen the forces for continuity.

All along the process and contingent on the specific needs of the situation, different specialist advisors can be very useful in guiding decision makers through succession. Like the decision makers they serve, succession service providers prefer continuity in succession. Advising for continuity compliments the current leadership on the job they have done—advising change would risk discrediting them; advising for continuity also maintains the service provider's relationship with the company and opens the door to new business. The succession planning process such as it prevails in business today allows for the possibility of change, but is built upon structural and institutional bases that favor continuity.

2.1   Succession Research

In recent years, business thinkers have been at the forefront of work on succession. Although always of central importance to historians, succession does not speak to the fundamental concerns of political scientists, appears as an outcome of political and social transformations and not as an explanatory variable in legal scholarship, and confirms rather than questions a number of tenets of psychology. Business makes use of the knowledge bases provided

---

[3] For a detailed description of what this entails, cf. Larcker DF, Tayan B (2010) Millionaire matchmaker: An inside look at CEO succession planning. Case CG-21, Rock Center of Corporate Governance, Stanford University Graduate School of Business.

by political history (more than political science per se) and psychology and works within the boundaries set by succession law, but, through application of the concepts over a large number of concrete cases, has developed its own unique take on the topic.[4] Where the focus of describing and theorizing about succession historically was on government, today it is on business, particularly on family businesses transitioning from one generation to the next and on founder-led businesses transitioning from the founder. As a result, knowledge about what it takes to manage succession in business has grown and matured.

One indication of the maturity of the field is the number of articles and books being published; another is the amount of attention the field draws from different branches of specialist knowledge. On both counts, succession in family and founder-led businesses fares very well. Despite the fact that the basic research insights—the importance of viewing succession as a process and the need to adapt the process to the context of the business—have been established for many years now and remain unchallenged, there is a steady stream of new work. Part of the reason for this continued output lies in the great variety of contexts encountered, not only economic but also strategic and cultural. Even more important is the fundamentally human nature of succession: every leader is different, and personal relationships play a major role in every succession process.

Going Against the Conventional Wisdom:
   Succession is all about psychology and relationships.—
   Although family psychologists are often at the forefront of consulting efforts to family and founder-led businesses trying to prepare for the succession question, succession research is actually much broader, including considerations of economic context, business condition, finance and taxes. The most experienced psychologists will, of course, be aware of this research and attempt to make it a part of their advice, but, in focusing on the psychology of succession, there is a danger of getting bogged down in conflicts that aren't relevant to the future of the business and can scuttle the whole process of succession planning. Thinking about succession can open a psychological can of worms, but it is important to always maintain a holistic view of what one is trying to accomplish.
   Certain personal relationships may be beyond repair, but where it is desired that the business continue, questions of governance, business strategy and financial viability still have to be addressed. Decision makers therefore need to walk a fine line between addressing the psychological questions raised by succession—and often only at the time of succession even though they may have been festering for years—and

---

[4] LeBreton-Miller I, Miller D, and Steier LP (2004) Toward an Integrative Model of Effective FOB Succession. Entrepreneurship Theory and Practice Summer 305–328.

letting these questions completely dominate the discussion. Everything is linked, and, in family and founder-led businesses everything is personal, but it is important to be able to ring fence the different issues and make progress on multiple fronts. It may eventually be possible to tie all the pieces together for the good of the family and the organization, but if it isn't possible, ring fencing will at least ensure that all the issues succession raises have been thought through.

Succession is always about individuals and their relationships, but it is never only about people. Those leaders and their advisors who reduce succession planning to questions of psychology and relationships are just as much in error as those who concentrate only on the legal and the financial. The former take an exaggeratedly personal view of succession, while the latter take an unrealistically concrete perspective in which physical assets are the measure of everything; both put the viability of the business at risk. The truth is multi-layered and complex; sometimes, a psychology-based analysis can suggest a new way forward for the business and the assets; conversely, in other situations, an asset-based analysis can lead to a new way forward for people and relationships.

Approaching succession as a context dependent process is much closer, in spirit, to King David than King Lear. A well-managed succession process is the opposite of an impulsive hand-over. In theory, treating succession as a process allows the leader and the organization to plan for and minimize many of the risks associated with succession: picking the wrong successor, provoking the opposition of key stakeholders, and, more generally, failing to prepare for the future. At the same time, treating succession as a process reinforces the tendency to favor continuity over change. Of course, the process can be (and is often) designed to explicitly consider alternatives outside the scope of continuity, but length and depth reduce the chance of decision makers agreeing on a radical departure.

Adapting the process and the outcome of succession to the context opens the door for change. Decision makers of a failing business, for example, have every incentive to take advantage of the succession process to initiate a change of direction or even to initiate the succession process with that objective in mind. The question is whether they will agree upon the meaning of economic and strategic developments and then have the force to act on the need for change. Someone or some group will have to drive the process in the direction of change. In larger family and founder-led businesses, this role typically falls to independent directors who may or may not be up to the essentially political tasks of rallying support and establishing the organizational basis for change. In the absence of such an external driving force, the process of succession takes on a dynamic of its own, subject to the structural, institutional and emotional forces for continuity described above. Somewhat paradoxically, then, thinking about succession in business provides for the possibility of adaptive change, but by failing to conclusively specify the agent for change, leaves the process vulnerable to the outcome of continuity, even in cases where continuity is not the right choice for the future of a business.

2.2   Best Practice

Given the amount of research on the subject and its broadly acknowledged importance, the finding that almost half of all family businesses do not have a succession plan is surprising.[5] The additional fact that almost half of those family businesses that do report having a succession plan in place admit that it is not properly documented suggests that succession planning is not widespread or thorough. Of all the likely reasons for this state of affairs, two appear particularly well born out: (a) many family and, by extension, founder-led businesses are more concerned with the business of doing business than with the business of succession and have trouble taking the time and effort needed to develop a formal succession plan; and (b) many leaders of family and founder-led businesses have such a strong personal tie to the enterprise that they prefer to indefinitely put off any consideration of the day when that tie will be broken; they plan to live forever. Where there is no succession plan, the terms used in this book, succession for continuity and succession for change, do not really mean anything. However, not having a succession plan also typically implies not making a structured effort to think about and prepare for future challenges. When succession does finally happen, continuity is the most likely outcome for businesses like these; in the absence of planning and preparation for change, continuity is the default option for any organization.

In those cases where a plan for succession is in place, one needs to differentiate between formal plans drawn up once and filed away and living documents referred to and updated on a regular basis. The former may or may not be taken out again when the discussion about succession heats up; the latter keep the succession discussion warm and ensure that the business takes the necessary steps to prepare for succession before it happens. Training and testing likely successors are absolutely essential aspects of a planned succession.

---

[5] Cf. 2014 PwC Global Family Business Survey of 2800 family businesses. Similar results are also regularly reported in other, more narrowly regional surveys.

In the case of younger candidates in particular, this can take many years, as various family members and other insiders are in effect given the chance to prove themselves. As important as it is, this kind of talent development is rarely part of the formal succession process per se. That process is launched when the leader feels the time has come (or the time is nearing) for him or her to consider stepping down. Where there is a board of directors in place, the leader will make the decision to launch the actual succession process in conjunction with the board and, where the board has a significant role in the business, give the board responsibility for managing the process. Where the board is weak or absent altogether, the leader will take over the management of the process. In the practical reality of family and founder-led businesses, no one will pull the trigger on the succession process without the current leader's explicit consent.

The details of the actual process depend on the type of organization, the context, and the characteristics of the departing leader. In any case, a seriously considered succession process takes a significant amount of leadership time, requires the input of a variety of voices and involves more than just the selection of a successor. As discussed in Chap. 1 above, thinking about succession often leads decision makers to contemplate the legacy of the departing leader and, subsequently, to formalize that legacy in statements of vision and mission that summarize the policies and norms underlying the past achievements of the business. In the same vein, the succession process also typically triggers reflection on the part of decision makers on the needs of the business going forward. This may or may not lead to a full-blown review of strategy (see Chaps. 5 and 7 for more on this point), but it certainly does focus attention on the traits required of a successor.

In general, legacy articulation and business review are seen as complements to the main show of finding and selecting a successor. Perhaps even more so than in the case of publicly listed companies without deep connections to their origins, decision makers in family and founder-led businesses are highly conscious of the importance, both symbolic and real, of the person in charge and therefore pay a great deal of attention to the choice of the new leader. In such businesses, as indeed in any organization with a concentrated power base, only very few people will be involved in the choice of the successor, typically the departing leader and his or her closest confidants. The actual selection process itself is therefore likely to reinforce a bias for continuity, as alternative candidates are weeded out in part on the basis of a lack of fit with the existing leadership. This is particularly true in the case of the succession of the founder—the founder, even more than a non-founder leader, is likely to look for a copy of himself/herself in a successor, and a lengthy, careful process of succession often serves the founder as an occasion to reflect on his/her contribution and to put in place people who will safeguard that contribution.[6]

Going Against the Conventional Wisdom:
Succession is all about finding the right person.—
Succession discussions often wind up focusing entirely on the person who is to succeed the departing leader. This is understandable, particularly in family and founder-led businesses where so much attention is on the person in charge. The danger is that an exclusive or even excessive focus on the person leads to less attention being paid to other issues of equal importance in succession. Worse still, a focus on the person to the detriment of a well founded analysis of the business may give rise to a false sense of confidence: once everything is in good hands, the business will take care of itself. Experience shows that even the most highly qualified individual will have trouble establishing him- or herself and leading the organization successfully if the conditions are not right and the person does not fit the growth trajectory of the business.

In some cases, preparation for succession does include a broad-based analysis of context and business, but the final decision will still focus only on the choice of the person. Even this kind of process holds risks that decision makers need to be aware of, principally the tendency to block out other information and rely on gut feel when it comes down to choosing one person over another. Gut feel is an essential part of decision-making in any organization and is especially important in family and founder-led businesses where people are not interchangeable, but, in the case of succession, gut feel should correspond first and foremost to an appreciation for the needs of the business.

Ultimately, the departing leader is the single most important player in the succession process. If the succession is to work for the business, he or she has to publicly anoint the successor. In other words, everything is stacked against the departing leader and his or her advisors making a neutral, impersonal evaluation of the candidates for succession. And yet, the departing leader has to put personal preferences aside and decide who and what is best for the business. That is a very tall order.

In addition to legacy, business and personal questions, succession in family and founder-led businesses also raises financial and legal issues, for the business and for the departing leader. Financial issues usually center upon shareholdings, dividend policies, and tax considerations, while legal issues include ownership and inheritance. Suffice it to say here (these issues have their own specialized treatments and differ by the country of incorporation of the business and the legal domicile of the persons involved) that financial and legal concerns in succession can be very complex. While it is definitely not best practice to focus the succession process exclusively on financial and legal as may have been more common in the past, it is also not acceptable to

---

[6] Wasserman N (2003) Founder-CEO Succession and the Paradox of Entrepreneurial Success. Organization Science, 14, 149–172.

treat these issues in a cavalier manner. As a general rule, the help of succession service advisors is very much appreciated in this area, and financial and legal may be the first areas where family and founder-led businesses seek help in managing succession.

Best practice in succession planning tilts the outcome of the process towards continuity. Although a fresh look at the needs of the business might point up the need for change at the top, the preparation of vision and mission statements to enshrine the legacy of the departing leader and the selection of a person who both fits the business and suits the existing leadership make it very unlikely that the succession process as currently constituted leads to change. Add to that length, complexity, and a restricted circle of decision makers and it becomes very difficult to see how succession for change can be engineered without rethinking the whole process: there are just too many hoops to jump through and too little diversity of opinion built in. Of course, succession for change is still possible, even under the current conventions of best practice, but it is not explicitly catered for and therefore unlikely.

2.3   Succession Services

A process that is as complex as the one described is very difficult to effectively manage without some help from the outside. This is where succession services come in to the picture. Succession has always attracted its share of counselors and courtiers, but the emergence of professional succession advice is a response to the specific and varied needs of modern business. Some succession advisors, such as consultants and executive search firms, are more interested in the health of the business per se, while others, such as private banks and tax specialists, are more interested in the wealth of the individuals involved. In some cases, advice is ordered à la carte, specialist by specialist, in others it is coordinated across the different stages and aspects of the process. When called upon, advisors typically work with the business and its decision makers over an extended period of time, making sure that all the bases are covered and building commitment to the ultimate succession decision. An important part of doing it by the book and following best practice is to engage the best succession advisors that money can buy and give them all the leadership attention they require to form deep insights.

> *Going Against the Conventional Wisdom*:
>   *Specialist advice should be sought on an as needs basis.—*
>   *In many cases, succession is the first occasion for a family or founder-led business to call on advisors to take a deep look at the inner workings of the organization and*

the governance arrangements of the firm. Of course, lawyers and accountants will have been consulted many times before for routine opinions—no business is small enough to do without completely without their input—but it is unlikely that any of this work ever touched upon questions of succession, family, or strategy. This mutual lack of experience works to the detriment of both the business and the advisor: the business gets advice that is based upon an analytical snapshot rather than a contextual understanding, and the advisor feels obliged to make undue use of pat solutions rather than properly adapted approaches.

For both sides, therefore, it is important to build a long-term relationship that precedes and follows up on the actual process of succession. The fact that the succession process impacts multiple domains—from business strategy to personal finance—and that all of the parts need to fit, puts an even greater premium on spending the time to establish confidence and trust. For this to happen, without the sword of succession hanging over them, the people at the top of family and founder-led businesses need to be persuaded that it is worth their while to work with different advisors as true consultants to the business, beyond the short-term utility of tranactional advice; advisors, in turn, need to get away from a charge as you go, transaction based approach and invest in relationships that may take years to yield profits.

Because it is such an emotionally charged occasion, succession is probably the least opportune time to start a relationship between family or founder-led business and advisor. Much better for the two sides to get to know each other slowly and without pressure, allowing personal bonds to form and commitments to be made. This recommendation goes against the grain of business people that would much rather focus on doing business and advisors who are often under pressure to reach sales targets. The ultimate proof of concept is in the results; for family and founder-led businesses, at least, there is too much at stake to make succession the occasion for first time experiments with advice and advisors.

Family and founder-led businesses are well known for being skeptical of advisors, and succession is one of the very few situations in which these businesses do frequently turn to outsiders for intensive consultation. Not surprisingly, therefore, succession is one of the main product offerings of advisors of all stripes, from consultants to private bankers. In general, advisors would prefer continuity in succession. Advising for continuity compliments the current leadership on the job they have done—advising change would risk discrediting them; advising for continuity also maintains the service provider's relationship with the company and opens the door to new business opportunities somewhere down the line. Indeed, in recent years and in response to the financial crisis that hit listed firms harder than risk averse family and founder-led businesses, many advisory firms have beefed up their offerings to these businesses.[7] The increased investment of resources on the part of

---

[7] Chapter 5 provides a detailed overview of the current state of succession services.

advisory firms further reinforces the predisposition for continuity in succession. For succession services, as well now, there is often just too much at stake to risk the potential rupture of succession for change.

2.4   Conclusion

Research in succession has come a long way since King David and King Lear. Although historical experience continues to play an important role, a disciplinary base in psychology and the substantial volume of research in business increasingly shape understanding of what it takes to manage succession. Best practice is quite clearly defined and includes legacy articulation, business review, and successor selection, in addition to the settlement of financial and legal questions. Thanks in particular to the research insights that succession is a process and depends on the context, professional advice has flourished, and succession has become much more predictable than it used to be in the past, when research was scarce and best practice vague. One size does not fit all, but there is a method for every situation. Method and complexity strengthen the forces for continuity. In a tightly orchestrated process with many established steps and multiple parties with a vested interest, there is less room for fundamental questioning and hence less likelihood for novel solutions to emerge. The succession planning process such as it prevails in business today allows for the possibility of change, but is built upon structural and institutional bases that favor continuity. When doing succession by the book, following best practice and hiring the best advisors, continuity is the expected outcome (Fig. 2.1).

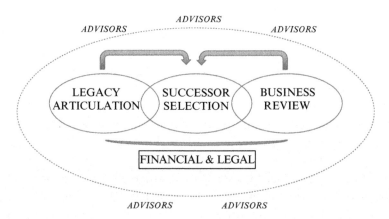

Fig. 2.1 Doing it by the book: a complex process for continuity

Part II

Succession for Change

This second, largely empirical part of the book presents an analysis of how competitive advantage has evolved over the last twenty-five years and examines the approaches being adopted by current business leaders, succession service providers and the next generation of leaders to address the change imperative in succession. One size does not fit all, and the variety of different efforts illustrates the magnitude of the challenge of succession for change.

3

The Change Imperative ... for Family and Founder-Led Businesses

Impermanence of Competitive Advantage. Over the last twenty-five years, business has gone through a dramatic transformation. At every level of analysis, from the macro of country rankings to the micro of firm activities, there have been significant shifts. Fundamental technologies related to ICT (information and communications technology) and biotechnology continue to evolve at such a rapid rate and affect so many areas of business that competitive advantage is always under threat.

Implications. Reinvention is hard enough when attempted by the existing leadership of a family business, or the founder of a business. Now add to that the need to think about succession as an occasion (if not the occasion) for considering a change of direction for the firm or the business.

This book is based on two premises: first, that the new primacy of innovative challenge fundamentally alters the rationale of succession in business, from ensuring continuityt to enabling change, and, second, that family and founder-led businesses find succession for change very problematic. In the following pages, we will take a closer look at these premises, putting the current state of economic competition into historical perspective and examining how family and founder-led businesses cope with transformative change.

The last twenty-five years have seen an unprecedented amount of upheaval in business. Many developing economies have joined the ranks of the developed economies; many industries of long standing have altered beyond recognition; and many famous old corporations have been absorbed or gone bankrupt. There is no reason to believe that stability will become the norm again anytime soon. Globalization and deregulation may be considered

© The Author(s) 2017
H. Korine, *Succession for Change*, DOI 10.1007/978-3-319-52120-6_3

one-time (albeit potentially reversible) effects, but technology development and entrepreneurship will continue to undermine competitive advantage everywhere. There are no safe havens from innovative knowledge recombination. From the most profitable industries, like pharmaceuticals, to the least profitable, like airlines, all are vulnerable. Even automobile companies, those powerful standard bearers of the industrial past, now confront novel offensives based on the technology of driving and the ownership of mobility.

Our era is witnessing a special constellation: both the environment of business and the practice of business are supporting change. Technological development and entrepreneurial drive are interacting to produce new products and new services. In response, the focus of research in strategic management has shifted. Whereas both the academic and the practitioner literatures once emphasized the importance of position, they now aim to explain change. From "value innovation" to "disruptive technology", the most influential business concepts of our age herald what one noted observer has called the "end of competitive advantage".[1] Of course, change also produces new industry leaders, and, in some respects, companies like Apple or Google appear even more dominant than General Motors and General Electric, their historical counterparts. The key difference is that the champions of today do not work to maintain position; they strive for continuous renewal.

In economic terms, the impermanence of competitive advantage affects family and founder-led businesses the same way as it affects all other businesses. The key difference lies in the importance of leadership identity: whereas strategies of publicly listed and other joint stock corporations are rarely explicitly tied to the identity of leaders, in family and founder-led businesses, strategies are often synonymous with the leadership—the name on the door. Consequently, succession for change is less difficult for corporations with a diverse group of shareholders. For family and founder-led businesses, succession for change means calling the identity of the firm into question. In family businesses that have been built over several generations, succession for change is up against loyalty to what the firm stands for; in founder-led businesses, succession for change struggles with undoing the founder's own achievements.

3.1   Impermanence of Competitive Advantage

Over the last twenty-five years (1990–2015), business has gone through a dramatic transformation. At every level of analysis, from the macro of country rankings to the micro of firm activities, there have been significant shifts.

---

[1] McGrath RG (2013) The End of Competitive Advantage. Harvard Business School Press, Boston.

The technology revolutions that kicked off in the 1970s and gathered steam in the 1980s prepared the ground for much broader change; the political revolution that saw borders open and regulation barriers fall in the 1980s and the 1990s opened up multiple new playing fields; and the entrepreneurial revolution that took root in 1990s took full advantage of the new technological and political conditions.

Looking back from 2015, the most striking indications of this transformation are the advances of new countries, new industries, and new companies. Comparing countries by ranking of their gross domestic product (GDP) in 2015 and 1990 shows that while China, India and the Republic of Korea have made huge gains (from 10th to 2nd, from 11th to 7th, and from 15th to 11th, respectively), Italy, Canada, Spain, and the Netherlands have experienced significant declines (from 5th to 9th, from 7th to 10th, from 8th to 14th, and from 13 to 18th, respectively).[2] Businesses from China, India, and the Republic of Korea benefitted both from the opening of their own vast markets and the opening of other markets around the world. Moreover, these three former developing economies established strong bases in information and communications technology (ICT), the new sector that has had the strongest effect on business growth, with China especially strong in telecommunications, India in software services, and Korea in information electronics. Contrast the performance of these three countries with that of Italy, Canada, Spain, and the Netherlands who did not benefit from a large home market opening, did not pursue newly opening markets to the same extent and did not manage to set themselves up as players in ICT.

The changes in country rankings find a clear echo in company rankings. Taking the Global Fortune 500 as the point of reference and comparing 2014 (the latest year for which the rankings are available) with 1995 (the first year of the rankings) shows several remarkable shifts[3]: (all) six Japanese companies have dropped out of the top ten, to be replaced by three Chinese companies; reflecting the developing world's appetite for energy, the number of energy firms in the top twenty has grown from two to eleven; and mobile telephony pioneers Samsung and Apple have come out of nowhere (221st and 422nd, respectively, in 1995) to replace old-line telephone operators AT&T and NTT as representatives of information and communications technology in the top twenty. Overall, only five companies, Wal-Mart, Shell, Exxon, Toyota and Daimler, have managed to stay in the top twenty over the entire period.

---

[2] The rankings of GDP (in current prices) are published annually, see http://knoema.de/nwnfkne/world-gdp-ranking-2015-data-and-charts.

[3] The data cited can be reviewed at http://fortune.com/global500/.

The rise of Samsung and Apple illustrates the new importance of the entire ICT sector. Of course, personal computers were already in general use by 1990, having superseded mainframes, and Microsoft (or rather Windows) was becoming a household name. The last twenty-five years, however, have seen the ICT sector deliver exponential growth and penetrate every aspect of modern life: not only has the internet become the basis of business and personal communications, it has also enabled continuous mobility and machine to machine interaction.[4] This could not have happened without significant investment in networks and technology development and visionary entrepreneurship. In fact, many, if not all of the companies that dominate the sector are creations of the last twenty-five years, and quite a few are still run by the founders (i.e. Google, Facebook, Amazon, etc.).

The share of the economy that is directly or indirectly attributable to or affected by the ICT sector is very large and growing. Internet and information based applications have penetrated every imaginable business activity: from pure research to final assembly, sales and after-sales service, today no single element of the value chain can make do without being connected. Even more importantly, the internet allows entrepreneurs to rethink and ultimately redefine many traditional business models: travel agency, banking, publishing (writing, music, and film), retail, to name just a few sectors that have been shaken by entrepreneurial firms making full use of the information super highway.[5]

A second major new area to emerge since 1990 is biotechnology, or the use of living matter in industrial products and processes. Biotechnology is age-old (e.g. fermentation), but only in the last twenty-five years has it started to gain major commercial importance. Like ICT, biotechnology is a source of both end products and enabling techniques, providing advances in healthcare, in agriculture, in energy, and in environment management. Like ICT, biotechnology stands for a complex and growing field of knowledge that allows for an almost infinite variety of combinations to drive innovation across fields.[6] Perhaps because capital requirements are larger, however, biotechnology entrepreneurs are less likely to stick around for the long haul and see their innovations through to market than ICT entrepreneurs. Many of the most successful biotechnology start-ups have either been taken over at an early stage by larger, listed players or eventually sold out.

---

[4] For a summary review of key innovations in the ICT sector over the last several decades, see http://www.alleywatch.com/2014/11/12-most-important-technologies-since-1990/.

[5] For an interesting description of the role played by the internet in changing how business is done, see http://www.mckinsey.com/insights/high_tech_telecoms_internet/internet_matters.

[6] For an overview and discussion of trends, see http://www.datafox.co/blog/2014/03/biotechnology-industry-analysis-key-players-future-trends/.

The ascent of new sectors like ICT and biotechnology represent one side of the story of our period; the other side is that of dying sectors and industries. The twenty-five years between 1990 and 2015 have also seen an acceleration of decline: newspaper publishing and photo finishing are the largest and most prominent examples, but recordable media manufacturing and DVD game and video rental are not far behind.[7] Even voice telephony is on the way out. Not coincidentally, all of the industries mentioned, and these were some of the biggest industries of the twentieth century, are being superseded by ICT and internet-driven applications. In other words, not even the most significant industries and companies are invulnerable to the accelerated pace of change.

So far, we have described shifts in economic activity among countries and among sectors and industries. The last twenty-five years have also seen significant *within* industry upheaval, with new players entering, established players exiting, and rankings shifting. In relatively new industries, like personal computer software, this is to be expected, and indeed we see that none of the top five firms in 1983 and only one of the top five in 1990 (Microsoft) even remain in business today.[8] Most of the early big players in hardware, i.e. Digital Equipment, IBM, and Sun Microsystems, have also fallen by the wayside (or at least exited the business), soon likely to be joined by more recent stalwarts like Hewlett-Packard and Dell Computer. In older industries, such as energy, steel, automobiles, trains, and cement, to name just a handful, increasing competitive pressure from globalization and technological development has led to widespread consolidation. Service businesses have not been immune from this trend: the banking, insurance, and advertising industries of today are much more highly concentrated than they were twenty-five years ago. The same holds for management consulting and audit, where the number of leading firms was small to begin with and has become even smaller.

At the level of the individual firm, too, change has been significant, even for the biggest and most established. The firms that have successfully navigated the last twenty-five years look very different from what they used to look like, with a different business mix, a different geographic orientation, and a different value chain. Thus, erstwhile product giants like IBM, Siemens, or ABB have moved to favor service over product offerings; formerly domestic or regional players like Cemex, Renault, or Tata

---

[7] An updated review of declining industries can be found at http://www.businessinsider.com/the-10-fastest-dying-industries-in-america-2012-4?op=1&IR=T.

[8] See Campbell-Kelly M (1995) Development and Structure of the International Software Industry, 1950–1990. Business and Economic History, 24, 2, Winter.

have become global players; and companies like Procter& Gamble, Roche, or Shell, who used to do as much as they could in house now prefer to outsource or partner for activities running the gamut from development to distribution.

Changes in business mix, geography, and value chain at the firm level have in turn contributed to blurring industry boundaries. Changing the business mix often means competing on the turf of suppliers and distributors; enlarging the geography served can lead a firm to see and pursue complementary opportunities outside its traditional scope; and partnering to enhance the value chain can open up new opportunities for creating value that are not evident in traditional industry positioning. Industry focus becomes secondary to meeting emerging customer needs. As mentioned earlier, internet applications have played an important role in enabling businesses to reach out to customers in new ways not constrained by industry boundaries. Even without the internet, however, intensifying competition in existing industries and changes in strategy in the pursuit of growth have been powerful drivers for rethinking the competitive playing field.

In looking for growth, firms have come to place ever more emphasis on innovation. Innovation can occur at many levels, from the simple cost-saving process to the complex new product offering; in the extreme case, innovation can lead to a new business model, that is to say an entirely new way of organizing the business. All types of innovation rely upon applying knowledge in new ways; more often than not, innovation is a matter of recombining existing knowledge. Recombining knowledge is less capital intensive than basic research, and the modern business firm is particularly well placed to see and act upon opportunities for knowledge recombination. Indeed, the firm-level changes in business mix, geography and value chain all contribute to facilitating innovation through knowledge recombination.

The last twenty-five years have seen fundamental shifts in the environment for doing business and, even more importantly, in the way of doing business. Environmental shifts like the opening of emerging markets and the emergence of new technologies represent one-time opportunities. Even once established, however, positions are not safe. Fundamental technologies related to ICT and biotechnology continue to evolve at such a rapid rate and affect so many areas of business that competitive advantage is always under threat. Taking advantage of opportunities for knowledge recombination, established firms and start-ups alike are constantly looking for new ways to innovate around the competition.

3.2   Implications for Family and Founder-Led Businesses

For family and founder-led businesses, the impermanence of competitive advantage has far-reaching implications. Of course, every family business and every founder-led business originates in an act of entrepreneurship. In the case of founder-led businesses, the original entrepreneur still leads the firm. In other words, family and founder-led businesses all have a history of addressing change and creating competitive advantage. The difficulty lies in doing so more than once—each time the context demands a new act of entrepreneurship. The developments we have described cannot be satisfactorily addressed by incremental adaptation. The challenge today is to enable the periodic reinvention of the firm (or of one of its major businesses).

By all accounts, many if not all family and founder-led businesses recognize the nature and appreciate the difficulty of the challenge of periodic reinvention. Several recent surveys explicitly identify change and the need to innovate to effect change as critical to the survival of family businesses.[9] The same research also acknowledges that change is especially difficult for this kind of firm, a point that is echoed in the views of the next generation of younger leaders who appear to be particularly concerned about change and diversification (see Chapter 6 below).

Of course, family businesses come in all shapes and sizes and are present in all industries, so generalizing is not easy. Among the largest family businesses, however, there is an overrepresentation in mining, manufacturing, finance, and retail, with more than 50% in these sectors.[10] These are capital-intensive sectors, where the patient capital provided by families has played an important role in supporting long-term investment. Traditionally, capital intensity has also served as a barrier to entry, protecting these sectors and their firms from the threat of radical change from the outside. As ICT enabled technologies and the firms that embody them make inroads into these established sectors, even the largest family businesses have to brace for fundamental changes to their business models. Recall our earlier discussion of the changes coming to the automotive sector: four of the world's eight largest family-controlled businesses

---

[9] See, for example, the 2014 PwC survey, http://www.pwc.com/gx/en/pwc-family-business-survey/assets/family-business-survey-2014.pdf; noted Harvard Business School family business specialist John Davis makes a very similar point in hbswk.hbs.edu/item/7364.html.

[10] This is shown in a recent study (2015) by the Center for Family Business at the University of St.Gallen, Switzerland in Cooperation with EY's Global Family Business Center of Excellence, of the largest 500 family businesses (defined as firms, private or listed, with over 32% family ownership), http://familybusinessindex.com/#table.

are automobile manufacturers (Volkswagen, FCA, Ford, and BMW), and their size will not be enough to protect them from knowledge-based innovation that goes to the heart of the very notion of mobility.

What about founder-led businesses? In the rapidly transforming ICT sector, entrepreneurs at the helm have generally followed one of two approaches: either, like the founders of Facebook and Google, they invest significant sums of money in research programs and acquisitions that add new technology capabilities without immediate commercial benefit and thus prepare reinvention; or, like Elon Musk and Martin Varsavsky or the Samver brothers in Germany, they sell out and start again in a new field, thus handing the challenge of reinvention on to the acquiring firms.

In less dynamic sectors, it is hard to make a general assessment of how founders address the challenge of periodic reinvention. Particularly enterprising individuals will start multiple businesses, adding new ones to the existing one(s) as opportunities present themselves. This is a pattern of serial entrepreneurship that is most common in emerging markets, where capital markets are less fully developed than in developed markets and the individual businesses draw financial benefits from being in a larger group. Other founders stick to the original business, but remain very much aware of the need to prepare for the future and tend to invest heavily in technology.

Going Against the Conventional Wisdom:
Family and founder-led businesses are less vulnerable to disruption.—
Family and founder-led businesses are often seen as lighthouses of steadfastness and stability. Where other types of firms lurch from trend to trend and from fashion to fashion, many family and founder-led businesses are indeed able to ride out cycles and resist fads. In other words, they are less vulnerable to bandwagon effects—but are they really less vulnerable to disruption, of the kind that fundamentally challenges the business model in use and changes the rules of competition?

Many long established family businesses operate in industries that rely heavily on fixed assets and/or brand investments: automobiles, mining, heavy machinery, electrical equipment, consumer goods, finance, retail, and hospitality, to name the most prominent. In the developing world, family businesses are also leading in infrastructure sectors, such as energy and telecommunications, where capital requirements are large. In theory, the need for vast amounts of steady capital in these industries creates entry barriers that protect businesses from disruption, and, for many years, they have indeed been protected from both competition and change. However, the availability of new ICT based approaches offers the possibility for getting around these entry barriers and upsetting established competitive positions without huge amounts of capital, or at least without the same heavy investment in fixed assets. Thus, for the first time in history, industries like automobiles or retail face challenges that go to the heart of how they do business, and fixed assets become a burden to flexibility.

Founder-led businesses that have been set up in the last twenty-five years, on the other hand, typically aren't anywhere near as well protected as their older family business counterparts that can rely on huge fixed assets or large brand investments. They are based on an entrepreneurial insight that puts existing technology to use to exploit a market opportunity. Here the rule of 'newer eats new' applies: whatever the sector, a technology based advantage is always temporary and vulnerable to the development of different, better technology. Many founder entrepreneurs are acutely aware of this vulnerability, an attitude that Andy Grove of Intel memorably summed up in the phrase "only the paranoid survive". Founders know that their businesses are living on the edge and that every succeeding wave of business model innovation represents a major risk to their survival.

Reinvention is hard enough when attempted by the existing leadership of a family business, or the founder of a business. So many questions have to be answered: does the firm have the necessary capabilities? If not, should these be bought in, or is this the time to sell out to a more capable rival? Will there be resistance to a change of strategy, and how might that resistance be overcome? Bringing succession into the picture complicates matters considerably. First of all, there may not be an obvious successor. Many family businesses and possibly even more founder-led businesses do not have a succession plan in place. Even if there is a succession plan, disagreement among the various stakeholders can make it difficult to implement. Now add to that the need to think about succession as an occasion (if not *the* occasion) for considering a change of direction for the firm or the business, and the problem takes on even larger significance. Major change is always difficult, and succession for change focuses attention both on the person of the successor and the need for change.

3.3   Conclusion

In this chapter, we described the current state of economic competition and stressed the impermanence of competitive advantage. At every level of analysis, from the macro of country-based competition to the micro of the products, geographies, and activities that firms engage in, the last twenty-five years have brought significant change. Given that the conditions that make competitive advantage impermanent, namely technological development and entrepreneurial drive, remain in place, we cannot expect the pace of change to slow. If even the largest, most technically advanced firms can no longer be sure of their position, then it is clear that we have entered a new era of competition in which every business must be ready for periodic reinvention.

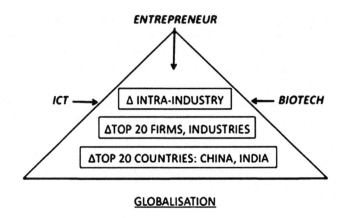

Fig. 3.1 The impermanence of competitive advantage: change at every level

We also showed that transformative change is high on the agenda of family and founder-led businesses. Family businesses, particularly those in the capital-intensive sectors that are predestined for patient family capital and have been protected by barriers to entry, face new kinds of competition based on innovative knowledge recombination that is capital-light, reducing their traditional advantage. Founder-led businesses that have emerged in the last twenty-five years are fully aware of the impermanence of competitive advantage. For these businesses, particularly if they are in very dynamic sectors or markets, the challenge is to keep up with the pace of change around them (Fig. 3.1).

4

Succession for Change in Current Practice

Sale. When the need for change coincides with the timing of succession, uncertainty and disagreement about the future of the business and the future leadership of the business may make a sale appear the least painful of options.

*Return of Family/Founder. The return of the family or the founder to the top leadership post once they have passed the baton represents the view that **only** the family or the founder can take the business forward.*

Outsider. Without agreement and support from the key players, even the most capable outsider is likely to hit a wall in trying to implement change.

Insider. An insider who has proven his/her entrepreneurial skill in building up complementary businesses has a better chance of transforming the firm upon succession if the organization has already moved in the direction of the desired change.

Succession for change implies that the decision-maker(s) recognizes a need for change in the business that goes beyond incremental adaptation and chooses to make succession a corner stone of that change. Recognizing a need for fundamental change in the business is never easy: there will always be questions about magnitude and about urgency. More avant-garde voices will advise action; more conservative voices will counsel caution. Combining change in the business with succession is also a matter of timing. The current leader may or may not be ready, from a personal point of view, to pass the baton. Potential successors may be too young or not yet experienced enough. Succession for change constitutes a critical entrepreneurial choice and always involves considerations of both the strategy of the business and the personal situation of the individua(s) concerned.

© The Author(s) 2017
H. Korine, *Succession for Change*, DOI 10.1007/978-3-319-52120-6_4

The impermanence of competitive advantage described in the previous chapter has had a significant impact on succession in family and founder-led businesses. Not wishing to engage in a new round of intense competition or lacking the wherewithal to do so, not a few families and founders have sold their firms. As far as the family or the founder is concerned, sale (or merger) hands the problem of succession for change off to the new owner. Sale of the firm has always been an option, of course, but it would appear to be more common today, not only among serial entrepreneurs who habitually sell and start something new, but also among established business families who sell and cash out. In the face of continuous change, the stigma traditionally associated with selling seems to have grown weaker, yielding to an appreciation of the sale as a legitimate business decision.[1]

The other way the impermanence of competitive advantage has directly impacted succession in family and founder-led businesses can be seen in the increase in the number of high profile cases in which the family or the founder returns to the helm to lead change: in the United States, Michael Dell has returned to privatize and re-ignite his eponymous company; in India, Narayana Murthy has taken over again at Infosys, in China, Li Ning has come back to steady his namesake firm, and in Italy, founder Leonardo del Vecchio succeeded his own successor at Luxottica. A succession process is put in place, a successor is found and installed, and then, under competitive pressure, the family elder(s) or the founder reasserts their prerogative to lead the business. In effect, succession is aborted. Comebacks of this kind are not new (i.e. the return to the head of Ford Motor Co. in 2001 of founder great grand-son William Clay Ford to stabilize a floundering ship, after twenty-two years of non-family leadership), but they appear to be becoming more common, especially when the founder of a business is still alive and able to reassume the executive role.[2]

Sale of the firm and precipitate return of the family or the founder represent extremes in succession for change, the former indicating a new start, the latter a failure of succession. Generally, when (and if) decision-maker(s) recognize the need for change, the succession process results in the choice of an individual who embodies the necessary transformation. In rare cases, the chosen successor is an outsider, a person without previous ties to the firm and

---

[1] The shame and emotional distress usually associated with a sale of the family business is perhaps best captured in Thomas Mann's novel, "Buddenbrooks". Although the business in question is no longer as successful as it once had been, the decision to liquidate, dramatically announced in Thomas Buddenbrooks' will, throws the whole family into turmoil.

[2] For a wide-ranging expert discussion of recent "return" cases, see http://knowledge.wharton.upenn.edu/article/the-pros-and-cons-when-the-ceo-returns/.

its leader(s), who, at least on paper, has the specific skill and the track record to lead the business in the desired new direction. More commonly, the family or the founder picks an insider, someone from the family or the inner circle who knows the firm well and shows promise for being able to transform the business. Pinning the hopes of the business on an individual—outsider or insider—is as old as succession itself. Family and founder led businesses have become more sophisticated over the years, however, in addressing the particular challenge of succession for change, bolstering the transition to a new leader with novel inter- and intra-generational support mechanisms as well as essential adjustments to governance. In the following pages, we describe the four different approaches—sale, return, outsider, and insider—presenting examples and discussing both the advantages and the pitfalls.

4.1 Sale: Objective or Anathema

On one end of the spectrum in thinking about sale stand serial entrepreneurs who can be defined as "those entrepreneurs who exit one venture before entering into a subsequent one."[3] In other words, exit or sale is an essential part of serial entrepreneurship. On the other end of the spectrum stand entrepreneurs and multi-generation family business leaders who have developed a strong emotional attachment to their firms and have great difficulties to even consider selling.[4] Between these two poles, there are multiple gradations, from the entrepreneur who would sell given the right combination of money and non-financial conditions to the family business leaders who decide to sell in order to free the family of the business.

The basic distinction—build to sell or build to keep—appears to reflect not only the amount of time and effort invested in a business, but also a fundamental psychological difference. Serial entrepreneurs and leaders who eventually sell their business take a more dispassionate view of what is good for the firm and what is good for the owner(s) than entrepreneurs and leaders who will not consider sale or will only consider sale as a last resort. It is not that the former care only about themselves or about money: a sales process that is satisfactory to the seller typically will also take into account the fate of the

---

[3] For example, as defined on p. 252 in Wright M, Robbie K, and Ennew C (1997) Serial Entrepreneurs. British Journal of Management, 8, 251–268.

[4] For a discussion of the value of emotional attachment to the firm, see Astrachan JH, Jaskiewicz P (2008) Emotional returns and emotional costs in privately held family businesses: Advancing traditional business valuation. Family Business Review, 21, 2, 139–149.

business itself, its employees and the broader group of stakeholders involved.[5] Sellers are able to see the business as separate from their person and their family name; business owners for whom sale is anathema, on the other hand, appear not to be able to make this cognitive and emotional separation: for them, the person/family is the business, and the business is the person/family.

There are multiple valid reasons to consider exit, both economically rational and emotionally persuasive. Economically, it may simply be a question of timing. Businesses in sectors that have peaked or are declining may never again be as profitable as they once were (see Chap. 3 above for examples). Of course, permanent decline is very difficult to predict with any degree of certainty, but there are by now so many contemporary examples of creative destruction, disruptive innovation, and long-term cyclical downturn that owners cannot ignore the very real possibility that something like this will also happen to their own business. In many cases where sale comes on to the agenda, entrepreneurs and family leaders have made the conscious decision not to invest in the next wave, either because they think it will be too difficult for the business as currently constituted or because they know they lack the ownership and management skills necessary to succeed in the new environment. Where major change that threatens the business is in the offing, the critical point to recognize is that things cannot go on as usual; exit may therefore be an option to consider.

Even if the survival of the business is not threatened, sale may be an economically judicious choice. Most entrepreneurs and many family business owners have the bulk of their assets tied up in the firm. At some point, the desire for diversification may drive an entrepreneur or (some of) the owners in a family firm to consider exit. The speed and extent of change in the business environment also plays a role in the desire for diversification. Whereas in the past, families and founders could be relatively sanguine about the risks of having all of their eggs in one basket, today's context of change can make diversification seem more prudent.[6] Finally, a founder or a family may come to the realization that success has been based on the founder's unique skills in putting together deals and decide that there is no long-term basis for continuing the firm's operations. Many emerging market business founders fall into this category—serial entrepreneurs who amassed a string of businesses, but "forgot" to sell. At some point, sale of at least some of the businesses thus put together becomes a logical choice.

---

[5] For a practical treatment of what a positive sales process can look like, see Burlingham B (2014) Finish big: How great entrepreneurs exit their companies on top. Penguin, New York.

[6] This point is echoed in Davis J, Pellegrin, J (2015) Managing the family business: Preparing to sell, Harvard Business School Working Knowledge, http://hbswk.hbs.edu/item/7757.html.

Succession itself can be a trigger for selling the firm. The family or the founder may not have a clear-cut successor in place. When the need for change coincides with the timing of succession, uncertainty and disagreement (where there are multiple owners) about the future of the business and the future leadership of the business may come to a head and make a sale appear the least painful of options.[7] In this case, economic rationality and emotional reason converge: without an agreed upon successor or in the face of ongoing conflict over succession, it may make more sense to sell than to continue.

Ultimately, the owner(s) confronted with succession for change need to put the advantages and the disadvantages of exit on a scale. The advantages are primarily economic: value realization (if the timing is right), diversification, and, in the case of disagreement over succession, freedom from ownership conflict for the business. While there may also be economic pitfalls (i.e. if the sale price does not reflect the long-term potential of the business), the disadvantages of exit have more to do with the emotional separation of the owners from the business and are therefore harder to quantify. Families, in particular, will miss the common purpose that joint ownership provides and will worry that the easy availability of money corrupts their relationships. By itself, a business is no guarantee for a common purpose. When owners or their offspring fundamentally disagree about the shape of the future, common ownership functions more like a constraint for the business and more like a straightjacket for the individuals concerned. A common purpose cannot be assumed, it needs to be negotiated. Ideally this negotiation is an ongoing process between and within generations, but, at the very least, it should provide the basis for thinking about succession for change. When change is an important prerequisite for survival, families and founders do their businesses a disservice if they exclude all consideration of the possibility of sale.

Going Against the Conventional Wisdom:
Selling the business amounts to a personal defeat.—
Having an emotional attachment to the business is not wrong. On the contrary, it is hard to imagine making the sacrifices involved in founding a business and keeping it in the family without an emotional attachment of some kind to the product, the organization, and the people. Nonetheless, it is important to try to separate the emotional from the economic. In holding on to the business in the face of economic logic against doing so, founders do not do their successors a favor, and the older generation of a family business do not make life easier for the next generation. Indeed, in some cases, the next generation may wish that their predecessors had the courage to sell when the time was right, rather than burdening them with the filial duty to carry on. Paradoxically, not selling may turn out to be selfish.

---

[7] See http://www.thefbcg.com/The-Right-Reasons-to-Sell/.

Selling the business should be considered as a business decision. In a context of continuous change, selling at the right time may be the best thing to do, especially in those cases where large investments are required to navigate the next stage and the successor generation does not agree on the steps to be taken. The question every leader needs to ask is whether the business will be better off under different ownership/different corporate parents. Metaphorically speaking, no matter how good the child, he or she may not be able to develop fully unless put in the care of the right parents. There may come a time when the business can only develop further if placed in new hands.

To even make it possible to consider selling the business in an orderly, dispassionate manner, a process needs to be put in place that allows each succeeding generation to decide for itself on whether it wants to keep or to sell the business (or parts thereof). Such a process should be built around a shareholder's agreement that specifies how, when, at what price and to whom shares can be sold and should not be so restrictive as to practically prevent the next generation or members of the next generation from selling. Here again, the concept of the hand from the grave is important—the hand should support, not get in the way of following generations from making their own decisions about what is best for them and what is best for the business.

4.2   Return of Family/Founder

The sale of the business represents the recognition that the family or the founder is no longer the owner best placed to take the business forward. The return of the family or the founder to the top leadership post once they have passed the baton, on the other hand, represents the view that *only* the family or the founder can take the business forward. The challenge of guiding a firm through major change can prompt a sale; it can also prompt a comeback of family or founder, years after they have passed the baton to a successor. The phenomenon of the old leader(ship) returning to power is not unique to business or even family and founder-led business, although it would appear to be more common in these types of firms. In the annals of contemporary listed companies without a family or founder link, there are comebacks like that of A.G. Lafley at Procter and Gamble or Myron Ullman at J.C. Penney. In twentieth century politics, we have the prominent examples of Churchill, De Gaulle, and Ben-Gurion, who each came back to lead their countries in answer to the call of crisis. What these returns have in common is a situation that requires dramatic action to save or at least renovate the organization.

The most famous case of the old leader(ship) returning to power in family and founder-led businesses is of course that of Steve Jobs' renaissance at Apple, the company he co-founded in the 1976, was forced out of in 1985 (although he remained a major shareholder) and came back to lead again in 1997. Although Jobs' return to Apple is unusual in several respects—the length of his separation from the firm and the degree of success his return generated—it typifies the logic behind the comeback of a leader. When Jobs returned in 1997, Apple was in deep economic trouble and faced a leadership vacuum; at the same time, the firm still had a unique combination of skills (in developing both hardware and software). Moreover, unlike his successors (first Sculley, then Spindler and, finally, Amelio), Jobs had the ability to develop a powerful vision, mobilize the firm's skills behind that vision, and convince customers and investors. In other words, Apple needed a turn-around, and Jobs was perhaps the only person with the requisite market competence and internal as well as external credibility to save the company.

The Jobs/Apple example notwithstanding, families and founders returning to executive leadership of the firms they gave birth to cannot be assured of success. While they may be able to rally the support of both employees and external stakeholders and are therefore able to make bold moves, their vision of the future may not prove correct. Just because they had it (the market) right the first time does not give them any guarantee of getting it right a second or third time. As importantly, the return of the family or founder overturns the succession process and makes the company vulnerable to all the side effects of a concentration of power: tunnel vision, infighting, talent flight, etc. On his second go-around at Apple, Steve Jobs himself recognized the importance of putting in place a succession process that would make the firm independent of its founder. Over the last seven years of his life, he spent a great deal of time and effort strengthening the firm's leadership team and reinforcing the firm's culture. He did not want the firm to have to rely on another comeback.[8]

The return of the founder or the founding family is related to the inability to let go displayed by many great leaders and discussed in Chap. 1 above.[9] Like the decision to stay on, the return can only be a temporary solution, if the firm is to outlive its founders. Most returning leaders say that it will only be for a short time, until the ship can be stabilized, or until a new leader for

---

[8] Interestingly, from the point of view of this book, the succession of Jobs appears to have been structured in such a way as to ensure continuity after his passing. His successors, Cook, and, in the background, Ives, have carried on the work of Jobs with little change (except, perhaps, in the matter of dividend policy). This is not surprising, given the success of the company at the time of transition. Succession for change is more likely when change is clearly necessary. It remains to be seen how the post-Jobs leadership will deal with (or themselves create) major upheaval in the industry.

[9] On the difficulty of replacing great leaders, see Lawler EE III (2011) Sustainable leadership: The problem with iconic leaders. Forbes, April 18.

change can be found. If the family or the founder have lost confidence in the leader and feel they have to return to an executive role, it is not only because of changes in external circumstances (read unforeseen market conditions); it is also because their plans for succession have failed. Perhaps they chose the wrong person; more likely, they sought continuity in succession, when in fact the business needed succession for change. If the founder or the founding family does come back and manages to reestablish the business, then it is absolutely imperative that they get succession right the second (or third) time around! This means they have to clearly limit their stay at the top and use the time to build a succession process, for continuity or for change.

Going Against the Conventional Wisdom:
If the family or the founder returns, something is wrong with governance.—
In general, the involvement of family and founder is a good thing. What it really means is that the owner(s) are taking care of their assets. The transition to non-family management is usually heralded as a step in the professionalization of a business. However, it can also imply that the family does not have an adequate successor in readiness, or, more dramatically, has lost interest in the fortunes of the business. Therefore, when the family or the founder is prompted by business reasons to return to the helm, it is not necessarily a bad sign, indicating de-professionalization or panic. Rather, the return, if well explained and supported by strong governance, can be just the push the business needs to make vital strategic changes.

Because a precipitate return of family or founder is also an indication that the succession process has not produced the expected results, such a return should be the occasion for rethinking succession and the governance of the firm. In particular, the succession process needs to be examined as to how well it incorporates the strategic challenges faced by the business: what kind of leadership has the mindset and the credibility to drive change? From a governance point of view, the succession process should address the evolving roles of family and founder, the financial concerns of shareholders, and the positions of non-family managers. An independent board of directors can be very helpful in guiding the firm through such a governance review. If these steps to revise the succession process are taken, a return of family or founder can actually be an opportunity for strengthening strategy and governance in the firm.

Once the business is on the right track again, owner(s), that is to say family or founder, need to agree to a process that institutionalizes succession for change. The owners will and should always retain the option to step in and take over. Again, ownership concern and involvement are good for a firm. However, a return of family or founder should only occur under clearly defined conditions and following a process that has been agreed upon by the major stakeholders. Succession is always an occasion to reorient the business; better that succession for change happens in a way that has been carefully prepared than in a knee-jerk manner.

4.3   Outsider: Not Destined to Fail

In the annals of succession research in family and founder led businesses, the case of Disney serves as a reference for illustrating both the advantages and the pitfalls of choosing an outsider to lead change. Only by finally breaking the long line of internal successors to Walt Disney in 1984 and investing Michael Eisner with the shareholder support to fundamentally change the direction of the firm, so the analysis goes, was Disney finally able to move forward, after *eighteen years* of indecision and infighting—founder Walt Disney died in 1966.[10] As much as he was praised for bringing about change, however, Eisner himself was later criticized for destroying the company's soul (and eventually forced to step down in 1995). That's the outsider/insider dilemma in a nutshell: in some cases, an outsider is needed to break deeply embedded resistance to change in family and founder led businesses; at the same time, an outsider tasked with transformation runs the risk of failing to understand and maintain what made the firm special in the first place.[11]

In the case of Disney, Eisner was able to accomplish a great deal in the way of strategic change before he ran afoul of the outsider's curse. After floundering for so long under a series of insider successors, the organization was ready for a fresh start. Few outsiders who immediately followed family or founder leadership have been as successful; on the contrary, many have not been able to bring about the transformation they were put in place to lead. Think John Sculley who followed Jobs at Apple or, more recently, Terry Semel who followed (and was replaced by) founder Jerry Yang at Yahoo! as typical cases. This is why an outsider, defined above as a person without previous ties to the firm and its leaders, is only rarely chosen to directly succeed family or founder, even if major stakeholders—and they often include the founder—recognize that change is necessary and outside leadership might be beneficial. The best track record in the world is often no match for the internal culture clash and power struggle the appointment of an outsider can lead to, particularly if the outsider is directly succeeding family or founder and has to undo some of their achievements to reposition the firm.

Why then do a few family- and founder-led firms nonetheless appoint outsiders to top leadership positions? In some cases, they do not have a choice,

---

[10] The Disney succession story is recounted in detail in Stewart JB (2005) Disney War. Simon & Schuster, New York. For a short summary, see also Following a Founder—Issues of Transition and Continuity in Family Owned Businesses, Center for Applied Research, 2009. http://www.cfar.com/sites/default/files/resources/BN_Following_the_Founder.pdf.

[11] The newness argument is summarized and tested in Weng DH, Lin Z (2014) Beyond CEO tenure: The effect of CEO newness on strategic changes. Journal of Management, vol. 40, no. 7, 2009–2032.

for no capable internal successor exists.[12] In other cases, the idea is to send all stakeholders—internal and external—a clear signal that change is on the way. Thus, one hundred year-old Japanese spirits giant Suntory recently made the unprecedented choice of giving an outsider the top job, for the specific purpose of leading a push for globalization. It can work. Both the new leader and the outgoing leader have to be very clear on their positions, what they will do and what they will not do. Both sides have to carry out their due diligence processes with great thoroughness to avoid surprises and misunderstandings. Most importantly perhaps, there has to be agreement about and support for—among family members in a family business and from the founder in a founder led business—what the outsider should accomplish. Without agreement and support from the key players, even the most capable outsider is likely to hit a wall in trying to implement change.

> *Going Against the Conventional Wisdom*:
>   *Bringing in an outsider never works.—*
>   *In some cases, an outsider may be needed to drive transformation of the business. Particularly where the managerial skill base is narrow and the culture is ingrained, only an outsider may have the necessary perspective to lead the business into a new domain. Of course, a new domain does not automatically spell success; on the contrary, the number of businesses that have failed in efforts to enter new domains is larger that the number of businesses that have succeeded in doing so. The issue is really one of urgency. If the business has no real strategic choice but to transform (sale is always a possible ownership choice) and actual members of the leadership team do not have the competence or the vision, then an outsider is the only viable possibility. The outsider may still not work out, but without the outsider, such a business has no hope of transforming and successfully navigating a new domain.*
>   *If an outsider is chosen, even more than if an insider is chosen to take the top job, major stakeholders have to agree explicitly on the person and on the goals, committing also to investing in new technologies and new markets. There can be no holding back or making side deals to protect particular interests in the event the outsider fails. Bringing an outsider to lead change is a dramatic step, and it can only have a fighting chance of working if family and founder in particular unreservedly stand behind the new person. Advisors to the process, board members and succession service professionals typically play an important role in bringing in an outside leader; they have to go the extra mile of making sure that everybody is on board with the decision.*
>   *The outsider in turn has to be the kind of person who diligently works to understand the particular challenges of the business, the culture of the firm, and the personal motivation(s) of the owner(s). Ideally, this is even a person who has had previous experience in coming in to replace family or founder leadership and hence is well aware of the particular challenges this entails. Not infrequently and rightfully*

---

[12] As noted above, not having a suitable successor can also be a reason to sell the business.

so, such a professional will demand assurances of stakeholder support up front. The odds are stacked against an outsider, but it is not mission impossible. Urgency, stakeholder commitment, and individual strength of character strength can, in combination, be a recipe for achievement in building succession for change on the shoulders of an outsider.

4.4   Insider: Not Destined to Succeed

In family and founder-led businesses, an insider, someone from the family or the inner circle who knows the firm well is more likely to succeed to the top post than an outsider. As the story of Disney illustrates, an insider is also more likely to stand for continuity than for change.[13] The Ballmer years at Microsoft (2000–2014) tell a similar tale of missed opportunity to transform and stagnation. The insider has the advantages of intimately knowing the firm and (usually) being able to count on the support of the family or the founder; he/she has the corresponding disadvantages of not knowing enough about the world outside the firm and being too close to the family or founder. As a result, an insider tasked with change rather than continuity will struggle. Change requires both internal strength and external openness. The question then becomes how best to prepare an insider for succession for change.

Traditionally, the scions of family businesses were seconded to friendly institutions for professional development. The training they received in banks, audit firms and law offices was supposed to prepare them for taking over the affairs of the family business and cement the relationship between the family and its partners. Over the years, it has become common practice for would be heirs to gain further experience and credibility by establishing the beginnings of a career outside the family business, returning only after making a name for themselves and perhaps earning a higher educational qualification. The objective of all this preparation is to give the members of the next generation who are interested in assuming responsibility for the family business a broad base for doing so. In the ideal case, the learning gained outside the family business can be used not only to support the business, as it exists today, but also to prepare it for the future. In other words, the seeds for change readiness can be sown early on in the career of the next generation of leaders.[14]

---

[13] Although it is important to note that insiders have been found to be more likely to promote innovation than outsiders, see Balsmeier B, Buchwald A (2015) Who promotes more innovations? Inside versus outside hired CEOs. Industrial and Corporate Change, 24 (5) 1013–1045.

[14] For a more complete description of the early years of the next generation's training and the logic behind it, see Lansberg I (2007) The tests of a prince. Harvard Business Review, September.

Inside the company, potential successors can get experience that is useful for change by starting and/or running new businesses in fields that develop the capabilities of the firm and promise growth. Indeed, in some families it is standard practice to give the next generation the funds and the opportunity to try out new areas. Similarly, in successful founder-led businesses, surplus capital is often invested in adjacent fields, and members of the inner circle of the founder(s) are given the chance to run these new offshoots and thereby display their mettle. This form of diversification serves multiple purposes: on the one hand, the firm is given a broader (and hence less vulnerable) base to stand on, improving prospects for survival and future growth; on the other hand, insiders with the potential to succeed to the top position are given a chance to prove themselves under competitive conditions. Both the firm and the individuals involved are thus in theory better prepared for leading change.[15]

This kind of succession testing is not without its pitfalls. For one thing, the new businesses entered may not be big enough to compensate any decline in the core business and may not even be relevant to the evolution of the core business. Even worse, the new businesses may be seen as places to park family members and friends of the founder, giving them something to do while they are waiting for succession. It is therefore critical that the new businesses be established in areas that can really advance and challenge the core business. If they do not gain scale and impact within a reasonable time frame (depending on the economics of the business), it is a clear indication that the efforts to evolve the portfolio of the firm are stalled and/or that the people running the new businesses are not up to the job and should not be considered for succession to the top job.

In developing new businesses and testing new leaders, it is important to keep in mind that the organization itself also needs to evolve. An insider who has proven his/her entrepreneurial skill in building up complementary businesses has a better chance of transforming the firm upon succession if the organization has already moved in the direction of the desired change. This means that the new businesses upon which the future will be based have been given priority and that the processes and incentive systems have been adapted to make change easier. With the ground thus prepared, succession for change becomes a natural next step for the firm, rather than a sudden redirection that pins all the hopes of the firm on one person.

---

[15] The Mulliez family's well documented practice of starting multiple new businesses (i.e. Auchan, Decathlon, Boulanger, etc.) and using them as training grounds for future executives (both family and non-family) fits this model of preparing for succession particularly well, see Connil Y, Crawford, RJ, and Bennedsen, M (2015) "The Mulliez Family Venture", INSEAD Case, 315-140-1.

Going Against the Conventional Wisdom:

With an insider, you always get continuity.—

It is the rare insider who can develop and maintain an outside perspective. This is why the insider is the obvious choice for continuity, and even when change is the desired outcome of some, the compromise choice of an insider for change often merely reinforces established ways of doing things. There are exceptions, of course. In a family or founder led business, an inside successor can be groomed for change. On the one hand, this involves allowing the individual to build outside and inside experience in businesses that are not related to the core. Again, the point for the potential successor is not to dabble, but to build a real track record and prove the ability to realize major change. It is also important that the outgoing leader not merely states his/her support of the insider who is to stand for change, but actually launches the process of transformation before stepping down. This can take many forms, a new strategy, a major acquisition, or a large investment in technology. Departing leaders who choose insider successors for change need to prepare the organizational ground.

If the desired change is given credibility by the departing leader's actions, and the organization already has experience in successfully adapting to change, then an insider succession for change has a much better chance of working out. This is the method the French entrepreneur François Pinault demonstrated so successfully in transforming the diversified holding company PPR into the fashion house Kering, while over the same period of time preparing and anointing his son, François-Henri Pinault, to run the transformed company. Although François-Henri had worked in the parent company for a long time, he stood for a way of doing business that was different from his father, focused on building brands rather than making deals. In effect and before handing over the reins, the father re-engineered the firm to adapt to a changed environment and to match his son's leadership skills.

The most effective insiders for change are those who can maintain an external perspective—before they accede to the top job and afterwards. This implies an ability to develop and grow contacts in different milieus and with many different kinds of interlocutors outside the organization. As an individual rises up through the corporate hierarchy, having this kind of outside life becomes harder and harder. After years as an insider, only very few individuals still have an external perspective that is fresh and continuously renewed. This is the kind of insider who can lead succession for change.

4.5   Conclusion

The increasing incidence of return of the family or founder indicates the extent to which family and founder led businesses are struggling to address succession for change. By definition, return of the founder can only be an interim solution, and return of the family only makes sense if the family has the requisite management talent within its ranks. Either way, precipitate

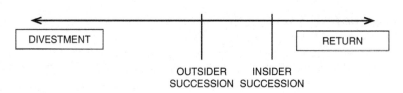

Fig. 4.1 Opposite extremes of succession: from divestment to return

return highlights the need to develop a better succession process. Ironically, then, the competitive challenge of dealing with faster and more fundamental change means stepping up long-term preparations for succession. Just because markets and technologies are transforming at an unprecedented rate, does not mean that family and founder led businesses should have a knee-jerk approach to succession. On the contrary, to be successful, all of the alternatives to return—sale, outsider succession, and insider succession—require time and commitment. A successful sale will have involved a variety of stakeholders over multiple stages; outsider succession, to have a chance to work out, must be supported by the majority of shareholders; and effective insider succession depends on giving potential successors multiple opportunities to prove themselves under market conditions.

Succession for change has to be put on the agenda of decision-makers, and the various possibilities need to be explored and prepared. The timing of major challenges is not predictable, so the firm must continuously question both the adequacy of its strategic positioning and the suitability of its leadership and their potential successor(s). Change readiness is what is needed, not only in the organization, but also at the top, and perhaps most critically, at the level of the next generation of leaders. Before we take a closer look at the next generation of leaders, we want to survey the state of succession services. How do professional advisors to family and founder led businesses look at the question of succession for change? (Fig. 4.1)

5

The World of Succession Services

Overview. Both the players and the resources invested have grown significantly since the financial crisis of 2008. Advisors who had traditionally concentrated on working for publicly listed firms shifted some of their attention to family and founder led businesses.

Recent History. The last three decades correspond to major developments in the sector: the 1990s to the explosive growth of trusts and the advent of psychologically trained family business consultants, the 2000s to the establishment of family offices and the proliferation of specialist wealth management offerings from banks, and the present decade to the rise of general consultants offering a strategic perspective.

Outlook. Family and founder-led businesses around the world today expect sophisticated, specialist advice on succession, but that advice has to be grounded in an understanding of the challenges faced by the business. As a sector, succession services are evolving from an almost exclusive emphasis on succession for continuity, as practiced in the 1990s and much of the first decade of the 21st century, to a more balanced view that includes the possibility of succession for change.

The emergence of the modern sector of succession services is an outgrowth of the needs of family and founder-led businesses that were large enough to outlive their founders. Throughout history, decision-makers have sought advice from counselors and courtiers on the question of succession, but it is the complexity of succession in business today that makes it necessary to call on a broad set of specialized professionals. Gone are the days when a banker or a lawyer could be counted upon to know (or find) all the answers. Succession in family and founder-led businesses touches on a variety of difficult questions: strategic, legal, financial, and psychological—questions for the firm and questions for the individuals concerned, both leaders and successors. First of all, leadership succession has implications for the strategic direction and the governance of the firm, as a new leader may or may not continue with the choices and policies of the old leader. In the closely held firm, where leadership is also associated with principal ownership, the legal and financial aspects of succession are very important. Psychological questions, finally, concern the retiring leader who has to accept a new role in life as well as the successor(s) who has to grow with the opportunity to lead.

The sector of succession services caters to all of these needs.[1] However, not every firm looks for this kind of advice. In fact, founders, in particular, are notorious for not concerning themselves with succession planning, preferring to get on with the business of doing business instead. Of those firms that do seek out help, some start their thinking about succession in discussions with bankers or lawyers; others take a more comprehensive view from the outset and speak to consultants with the reach and breadth to give initial cover to all of the issues. Either way, once advice is sought, decision-makers usually recognize the complexity of the matter and seek out multiple specialists. For a family firm that has successfully handled succession on several occasions, succession may become increasingly standard, but for first-timers passing from the founder to the next generation and for firms where the process is in dispute, succession represents a major commitment of time and resources.

5.1   Overview

It is difficult to map out and estimate the size of the succession services sector. The sector includes so many different players, and, like the proverbial blind men touching the elephant, each one of them only has a partial view. What the experts I talked to in the preparation of this chapter do agree upon is that both the number of players and the resources invested have grown significantly since the financial crisis of 2008.[2] Specifically, advisors who had traditionally concentrated on working for publicly listed firms found that source of business growth had largely dried up and therefore shifted some of their

---

[1] Strike VM (2012) Advising the Family Firm: Reviewing the Past to Build the Future. Family Business Review, vol. 25, no. 2, 156–177.

[2] Our interviewees for this chapter included Peter Leach, Partner, Head of UK Family Enterprise Consulting, Deloitte LLP; Ivan Pictet, retired Managing Partner, Pictet & Cie.; Joerg Ritter, Partner and Co-Leader of the Global Family-Business Practice, Egon Zehnder; Roderik Strobl, Vice President, Crédit Agricole (Suisse) Conseil SA; and Tim Urquhart, representative of STEP.

attention to family and founder led businesses who had generally done a better job of weathering the crisis. Thus, firms as diverse as McKinsey, Boston Consulting Group, Goldman Sachs, Deloitte, and PWC have made family business a focus of their efforts in recent years, hiring professionals with relevant experience, publishing expert reports, and organizing events for business families and entrepreneurs.

Amorphous and fragmented are perhaps the words that best describe the succession services sector. Not all of the players active in the sector actually concentrate on succession. Estate lawyers, specialized tax advisors, and family business consultants do devote the bulk of their time to succession issues. Professional service firms with a more diverse base of business, however, typically also offer some form of succession advice, drawing upon the broad capabilities in their organizations, but do not make it the sole focus of their business. Banks and especially private banks are further players in the succession game, focusing on transactions resulting from succession and private wealth, but ready to provide a much more extensive palette of services. Family offices, finally, although specialized in wealth management, may also play a coordinating role for the family business in leadership succession.

Whereas many lawyers and tax advisors are mainly local, other providers are increasingly global, both in the customers they reach and in the services they can deliver. Over the last twenty years, globalization has produced a big number of successful new family and founder-led businesses, particularly from emerging markets, and many of these are now also starting to face founder to next generation succession questions.[3] Add to this number their counterparts from developed markets, where firms that grew during the boom years are now also on the brink of generational transition, and it is clear that the demand for succession services is healthy and growing.

Going Against the Conventional Wisdom:
   Succession services are the preserve of specialist firms with local roots.—
   A specialist firm with local roots, such as a law firm or an auditor may well still be the first port of call for the family or founder-led business seeking advice about succession, but it is rarely the only or most important port of call. Larger businesses in particular do not have to wait until succession is at the door to be noticed by big, international advisory firms, but are likely to have come into contact with them much earlier, when making a major deal, or setting up international investments, in

---

[3] For the special challenges of managing succession in the Chinese family context, see Tan WL, Siew TF (2001) Coping with Growth Transitions: The Case of Chinese Family Businesses in Singapore. Family Business Review, 14, 123–139 and Yan J, Sorenson R (2006) The Effect of Confucian Values on Succession in Family Business. Family Business Review, 19, 235–250.

other words when preparing specific transactions. The question for both sides is how a transaction services relationship translates into a succession services relationship— the first is based primarily on expertise and reach and has a short time window; the second is based primarily on confidence and trust and can take a long time to yield benefits. What is clear already is that family and founder-led businesses have more choice than ever before when choosing whom to work with on the question of succession.

Since the financial crisis of 2008, consultants of all stripes have sought to enter the sector of succession services, bringing to the table strategic analysis and global reach. Although the main experience of these firms has been with the issues of listed companies, they have been quick to ramp up targeted offers for family and founder led businesses. With so many players now vying for business, the space is highly fought over. So far, the general consultants' main effort has been aimed at getting in the door, so as to be ready for the succession discussion when it becomes relevant.

Gatekeepers such as board members and friends of the family or founder are key go-betweens for those advisors who do not yet have a relationship with the key decision makers, particularly in emerging markets or in remote areas of developed markets. As relationships strengthen, family members and founders are increasingly willing to open up their books and their hearts to advisors who are not local and have not known them for a long time. Nonetheless, cultural differences persist—between family and founder with an emotional stake in the business and dispassionate advisor and between locally anchored leader and global consultant.

5.2   Recent History

Hard to believe that a sector that today includes so many different offerings and draws so much international attention was as recently as the 1980s the province of local lawyers, accountants and bankers who, as a sideline to their main areas of activity, looked after the wealth of business families. More complex regulation, particularly in the fields of taxation and banking, increasing recognition of the interrelatedness of business and personal issues, and significant internationalization, coupled with the sheer growth in number and size of family and founder-led businesses, have made the succession services sector into what it is today: multiple dedicated firms (or dedicated departments within firms) with access to top notch specialist knowledge vying for the attention of a discerning group of decision-makers around the world who (in the case of the largest family and founder led businesses) have their own professional structures in place.

Like any other industry undergoing fundamental transformation, the succession services sector has gone through a series of stages, with requirements evolving and new players entering along the way. For the sake of convenience and at the risk of oversimplifying, we divide the transformation into three decade-long stages, the 1990s, the 2000s, and the present decade; as it happens, the decades also correspond to major developments in the sector, the 1990s to the explosive growth of trusts and the advent of psychologically trained family business consultants, the 2000s to the establishment of family offices and the proliferation of specialist wealth management offerings from banks, and the present decade to the rise of general consultants offering a strategic perspective. As we will show, while the first two decades under review reinforced the predisposition of family and founder-led businesses towards succession for continuity, the last decade has marked a subtle shift in the emphasis of succession advice, from succession for continuity to succession for change.

1990s—trusts and family business consultants: Already in the 1980s, but then increasingly so in the 1990s, the United Kingdom in particular, and common law countries in general, experienced strong growth in the creation of trusts for the management of succession in family and founder led businesses. The primary motivation for the creation of trusts was a fiscal one, to save on estate taxes as businesses were handed down from one generation to the next. In addition, the trust structure has the benefit of locking into place certain principles of how the firm is to be owned, run and disposed of, typically putting outsiders in place as directors of the trust and making it very difficult for descendents to change anything about the trust or the business. By protecting the wealth of the family business from the cupidity of both the state and the next generation(s), the trust structure offers a powerful instrument for ensuring the continuity of a family business. Already in 1991 trust and estate professionals got together to form the Society of Trust and Estate Practitioners (STEP), a professional association devoted to the education and certification of trust experts and, although the number of trusts created annually has declined since 2006 (as tax advantages associated with trusts have diminished), STEP remains a strong organization today, with over 20,000 members in 100 branches worldwide.

In parallel to the growth of trusts, but completely independent thereof, the 1990s saw the advent of psychologically trained family business consultants who came out of business schools to work directly with families on the emotional aspects of succession and governance. With plenty of anecdotal evidence and an increasing foundation of research to show that personal conflict was at the root of many failures of succession in family business, these consultants addressed an important area of concern that had hitherto either been dissimulated or left to the amateur mediation of close friends of the family. A few names from this period stand out and continue to dominate this specialized area of advice: John Davis of Harvard, Kelin Gersick of Yale, Ivan Lansberg of Northwestern, and John Ward of Northwestern. The work of these academics in bridging research and practice has had a profound influence on succession planning for family and founder-led businesses, making it emphatically clear that no legal or fiscal solution for succession can stand up to the destructive powers of a family that is disunited. For family business consultants, the starting point is always the emotional make-up of the family; the succession plan has to build on a thorough understanding of personal and family psychology.

At first glance, trust and estate practitioners on the one hand and family business consultants on the other would not seem to have much in common. What their synchronous growth in the 1990s does represent, in terms of the succession services sector, is the increasing importance of specialization. Where in the past, the personal advisor—typically a lawyer or a banker—of the head of the family might be called upon to give his or her opinion on a broad range of issues related to succession, the growth of specialized professional advice corresponded to a client need for more sophistication in succession services: the "hard" legal issues and the "soft" personal issues were becoming too difficult and too complex for the friendly advisor next door to competently address. If continuity of the business was to be ensured, and family business consultants who work to keep the family together stand for continuity as much as trust and estate practitioners who work to keep the business structure together, then professional help was needed.

2000s—family offices and wealth management: The trend toward specialization continued through the turn of the century. The apparatus of trusts became ever more highly developed ("bullet proof", in the jargon of its practitioners) and family business consultants grew in number, allowing for sub-specialization by issue category and geographic region. At the same time, family businesses recognized the need to separate questions of wealth and inheritance from questions of the business per se, and families with significant financial assets founded family offices that specialized in preserving the wealth of the family. Initially, the same people who managed the finances of the business also ran the family office, but very soon it came to be staffed with its own specialists, frequently former employees of banks and asset management firms. The number of family offices ("single family" for very large family fortunes, sometimes "multiple family" for investable assets of less than $ 300 Mio) has grown tremendously, with something over 400 in Switzerland alone at last count.[4]

---

[4] The discussion of family offices draws particularly on Faktor V (2013) New Family Office Governance. Difo-Druck GmbH, Bamberg, University of St. Gallen doctoral dissertation.

At least partially in response to the growth of family offices, specialists in wealth management (i.e. banks and investment firms) developed a product-based approach to dealing with family and founder-led businesses. In practice this meant that wealth managers moved away from the traditional relationship-based interactions with families and entrepreneurs and focused on selling investment vehicles to family offices. In effect, many banks progressively withdrew from the sphere of succession advice, engaging instead in a specialist-to-specialist dialogue about investments with family office investment professionals. The concentration on selling products improved the bottom line of financial firms in the short run but, in the longer run, left them cut off from the business relationships with the family that had once characterized their position in succession services. By shifting the focus of a large subset of succession services from succession advice about the business to products for preserving wealth, the emergence of family offices also reinforced the emphasis on succession for continuity in succession services. The bank could make good money advising the family office on how to preserve the family's wealth without getting in to the thorny issues surrounding succession in the business.

Although strictly speaking the family office is not (or increasingly less) concerned with the business or succession in the business, it has a direct line to decision-makers in the family and can function as a gatekeeper, determining who does and does not get the ear of the family. This has raised the difficulty of reaching decision makers and made the family office another actor that the succession services sector has to consider. Particularly when succession involves questions of restructuring or even selling (parts of) the business, the family office specialists with a mandate for preserving the wealth of the family will have a word to say. This means that succession services for large family businesses have had to become even more professional and specific in their offering, while dealing with an additional actor with a vested interest in continuity.

2010s—consultants with a strategic perspective: The financial crisis of 2008 hit publicly listed companies that had highly leveraged balance sheets harder than the generally more conservatively financed family and founder led businesses. Moreover, for several years after the crisis, economic growth was much stronger in emerging markets than in the United States or in Europe, and emerging markets are dominated by family and founder led businesses. As already mentioned in the industry overview at the beginning of this chapter, the aftermath of the crisis coincided with a "rediscovery" of family and founder-led businesses as important sources of revenue by many professional service firms and banks. Because succession is critical in closely held firms, all service providers have to address the issue in some manner. Thus, the general consultants who had previously only given little attention to family and founder-led businesses as well as the banks that had focused on selling investment products to family offices moved to beef up their succession related offerings.

From these players, we see the outlines of two distinct approaches: on the one hand, there are firms like Deloitte or PWC that are building the skills to offer a one-stop shop for succession services; on the other hand, there are firms like Egon Zehnder or the Boston Consulting Group who are using their specialization (i.e. executive succession or strategy consulting) as a point of entry into the larger question of succession in family and founder led businesses, ready to help the client work with and orchestrate a team of outside specialists.[5] The origins of the two approaches lie in the different capability bases of the firms—comprehensive for the would-be one-stop shops, rather more narrow for the specialist consultants. For either approach, access to decision makers is critical. Professional service firms have traditionally focused their client relationships on senior executives, not on owners or shareholders. Where succession in family or founder-led businesses is concerned, the owner(s) of the firm is the client. This is particularly true in emerging markets, but also plays a key role in Europe and the United States. Even where families have delegated responsibility for most activities to non-family managers, succession cannot be addressed without taking their views into account.

With the growth of family and founder led businesses around the world, the pie of succession services has gotten larger, but the field has also become more crowded. Today, specialists and generalists, established providers and newcomers compete side by side for the attention of decision makers. The proliferation of players leads to a buyer's market, but also makes it harder for decision makers to choose among advisors. In this situation, the personal contact to business owners plays a critical role in getting the service offering on the table.

Going Against the Conventional Wisdom:
   The search for a new leader is the starting point for succession advice.—
   While the person of the leader is primordial in any family or founder-led business, and succession services have to be able to reach the key decision maker, the change imperative in strategy requires a focus on the needs of the business. Theoretically, this gives an advantage to succession service providers who make business insight the basis

---

[5] Banks building up succession services also fall into the specialist category, with the difference that they are generally less interested in succession per se and more interested in the financial transactions (i.e. asset sales and wealth management) that may come out of a succession. In any case, a focus on compliance has made banks less willing to try any radically new strategies.

of their approach. However, speaking to the current leader about strategy change is a risky proposition, particularly for a firm that is attempting to enter a new market and does not have a long relationship with the client to look back on. In suggesting that the strategy that the leader has built, often over many years, needs to be reviewed, if not revised, the advisor is in effect also questioning the leader. That is why even those providers that count strategy as their primary expertise typically prefer entering the succession space on more traditional and less threatening platforms such as executive search or family psychology.

In other words, strategy questions typically become part of the service offering only after the advisor has entered the door and helped decision makers identify strategy as a key issue to consider in the succession process. The danger in proceeding this way is that strategic analysis and consideration of new business alternatives become afterthoughts in the succession process: nice to have, but not central. If succession is to be for change, however, questions of strategy have to be central to the analysis. Therefore, advisors who have the best interests of the business at heart sometimes have to take the difficult step of putting strategy first, even at the risk of alienating key decision makers. Fortunately, people close to the departing leader and, indeed members of the next generation of leadership can serve as bridges between the old and the new. Once in the door, it is the advisor's job to identify these people and make allies of them.

The job of advising on succession for change is fraught with danger. Many traditional succession service players will undoubtedly shy away from this kind of assignment or attempt to turn it into an assignment of succession for continuity. Succession for change plays to the particular strengths of the general consulting firm—business focus, integrated offering, broad reach—but making it work as a business proposition is a tall order. The only way for succession advisors to do so is to build strong relationships with decision makers and commit to being in the game for the long haul.

5.3   Outlook and Conclusion

Any form of succession advice to family and founder-led businesses has to cover multiple bases: legal, financial, and, perhaps most important of all, personal. More and more, succession service providers are also being confronted with the need to consider the strategy of the business itself. Either because a formal strategy analysis has preceded the inquiry into succession or because decision makers are concerned about the future of their business, strategy and change have entered the frame. Businesses have to address the increased speed of change on all dimensions, technological, regulatory and competitive, and succession service providers are asked to adapt.

How the providers respond to the need to consider strategic change in their work on succession depends on where they come from. In a trust, succession for change can only happen if the trustees are aware of the business need to transform and are willing to act on it. Accordingly, STEP is today putting more emphasis on business knowledge in the training it provides to trustees, who, as a general rule, come from a background of legal or accounting and do not start from a strategic perspective. Family business consultants, many of them with a business school background, are including basic principles of strategic analysis in their diagnosis of the situation of the family and the founder.[6] General consultants and specialist firms are giving succession mandates to partners with strategy experience or availing themselves of strategy expertise, in order to make sure that their advice on succession is embedded in the strategic reality of the business. In other words, every type of succession service provider, even the trustee put in place to uphold continuity is now making an effort to address the need to offer a perspective on succession for change.

Of course, the need to give strategy and change proper consideration is not the only development affecting succession services for family and founder-led businesses. Other priorities include continuing internationalization and, for both one-stop shops and specialists, seamless coordination of the different offerings that make up the succession package. However, internationalization and coordination are taking place in the context of a greater emphasis on strategy and change. Whether legal, financial, personal, or combined, the advice to the family or entrepreneur cannot occur in a vacuum, ignoring the future of the business. Family and founder-led businesses around the world today expect sophisticated, specialist advice on succession, but that advice has to be grounded in an understanding of the challenges faced by the business.

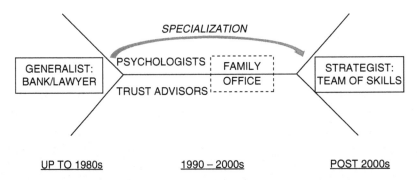

Fig. 5.1 The evolution of succession services

---

[6] See, for example, Carlock RS, Ward JL (2001) *Strategic Planning for the Family Business*. London: Palgrave Macmillan. More recently, Fernandez-Araoz C, Iqbal S, and Ritter J (2015) Leadership Lessons from Great Family Businesses, Harvard Business Review, April, put "strategizing about the future" and agreeing on "strategic goals" at the start of the succession planning process.

As a sector, succession services are evolving from an almost exclusive emphasis on succession for continuity, as practiced in the 1990s and much of the first decade of the twenty-first century, to a more balanced view that includes the possibility of succession for change (Fig. 5.1).

6

Next Generation

Changing Attitudes. On average, those who desire more control over their own lives and exhibit a higher propensity for entrepreneurial activity are **less** likely to want to succeed in the family business. Succession for continuity fails to attract enough potential successors of the next generation.

Next Gen Groups. In contrast to previous generations that did not look outside the inner circle for ideas, the next generation engages in open exchange with peers in other family and founder-led businesses and has something substantial to say about what constitutes best practice in matters of succession.

Networks of Families. Unlike the traditional method of giving potential successors a protected playground for trying new ideas under the umbrella of the existing business, cooperation between families on new ventures exposes the next generation to real world competition and represents a promising way to introduce succession for change.

The greater part of succession advice is aimed at the current generation of leaders. Inasmuch as it is the current generation that is making decisions about succession this would appear to be the sensible approach. However, making succession decisions without explicitly taking the perspective(s) of the next generation into account can be an important cause of trouble for all parties concerned, individuals and the firm itself. At a very basic level, it is important to avoid misunderstandings about the objectives of the succession process. Decision makers of the current generation and their advisors should not assume that the next generation holds the same views about what constitutes a meaningful career and about what business leadership requires. On the one hand, research shows that, as a whole, the (current) next generation (defined as those born after 1980) can be considered more self-centered and more self-

© The Author(s) 2017
H. Korine, *Succession for Change*, DOI 10.1007/978-3-319-52120-6_6

directed than previous generations.[1] This means that next generation leaders may be harder to groom and plan for—they are more likely to want to actively drive the succession process. On the other hand, the next generation is more open and a lot more networked than their predecessors, thus able to see many more opportunities for professional development, both inside and outside the business.[2] These differences between the current and the next generation of leaders necessarily affect succession: many in the next generation are less likely to passively accept a waiting game of leadership transition.

In this chapter, we discuss both the characteristics and the various activities of the next generation of leaders in family and founder-led businesses. While the summary of characteristics draws on secondary research, the description of what the next generation is doing is largely based on original research, conducted both in Europe and in Asia. We will see that openness and connectedness are not mere abstract accounts of the current state, but lead to novel group behaviors and networks for doing business that have a direct bearing on succession for change. Whereas previous generations, including the current generation of leaders, worked their way up without substantial contact to the successor generation in other firms, the next generation of today actively engages with their counterparts outside the firm, developing knowledge about succession and, in some cases, individually or even jointly with other members of the next generation creating new businesses that establish a basis for change. In a word, many in the next generation are doing, not waiting. This must have a profound effect on the time frame and the outcome of succession.

6.1   Changing Attitudes

One of the few established streams of research about the next generation in family and founder-led businesses concerns the intention to succeed. Thus, the comprehensive Ernst Young/University of St.Gallen benchmark survey (2012) of the next generation is able to draw on solid bases in social psychology and empirical application to conduct an extensive study of succession

---

[1] This point is made in numerous publications on the subject, popular and academic. For a research-based overview, see Twenge JM (2006) Generation me: Why today's young Americans are more confident, assertive, entitled—and more miserable than ever before. Free Press, New York. More recently and in a more popular vein, see Stein J (2013) The me me me generation. Time, May 20.

[2] The relationship between the availability of the technology for connecting and the incidence of openness and networking is reciprocal, and it is very difficult to separate one from the other. For more a detailed examination of this question, see Licoppe C, Smoreda Z (2005) Are social networks technologically embedded? How networks are changing today with changes in communications technology. Social Networks, 27, 317–335.

intention.[3] While confirming the conclusions of previous cross-sectional studies in several important respects (i.e. the importance of early introduction to the firm and extensive socialization), the study also presents a number of results that should give succession research pause. Most significant among these for our purposes is the finding that succession intention in the next generation is positively associated with less desire for control and less entrepreneurial efficacy. That is to say, on average, those who desire more control over their own lives and exhibit a higher propensity for entrepreneurial activity are *less* likely to want to succeed in the family business.

To the extent that succession today is increasingly about change and innovation, this is a worrying result. Could it be that those who intend to succeed are precisely the ones who are least predisposed to anticipate and drive change? Of course, caution is advised when analyzing any kind of large-scale, cross-sectional survey: sample bias, questionnaire construction, external validity, etc. And yet, when a study is built on proven metrics like this one is, the conclusions deserve attention. At least in the minds of a majority of participants, succession in the family business such as it exists today is not associated with the potential for making entrepreneurial change. The finding that less than a quarter of the members of the next generation surveyed actually intend to succeed in the family business reinforces this interpretation. If, as the generation focused research cited earlier in this chapter argues, the next generation is generally more self-oriented and wants to build its own proofs of success, then succession as it is currently conceived—succession for continuity—is not the right way. Not only does succession for continuity skirt the need to make the firm change ready, it also fails to attract enough potential successors of the next generation. Where are the potential successors of the next generation with the entrepreneurial qualities necessary to drive change? It is time to take a look at what the members of the next generation who are concerned about succession as usual in family and founder led businesses are doing about it.

Going Against the Conventional Wisdom:
Those next gens who want the top job are the best succession candidates.—
The intention to succeed can have a lot to do with obligation and a sense of responsibility—towards the business and for the family. Indeed, many members of the next generation in family and founder led businesses have been inculcated with these feelings from an early age. In Asian and Latin American contexts, parental

---

[3] Zellweger T, Sieger P, and Englisch P (2012) Coming home or breaking free? Career choice intentions of the next generation in family businesses, Ernst & Young/Universität St. Gallen. The complete study can be found under http://www.guesssurvey.org/PDF/2012/Coming_Home_or_Breaking_Free.pdf.

inculcation is complemented by societal pressure: for a "good" son (in most cultures, daughters feel less pressure in this regard), succession is the "right" thing to do. Thus, wanting to succeed may merely be an indicator of having to succeed. In the course of our research, we have met many members of the next generation in family and founder-led businesses who feel obligated to succeed, whether they want to or not. In some cases, the pressure is explicit, in others it is unspoken, but the general effect is the same: young people who feel a heavy weight on their shoulders and do not look forward to the future.

In our view, the obligation to succeed is not a good prerequisite for entrepreneurship and change readiness. Quite to the contrary in fact, it may be precisely those next gens who do not want to succeed, indeed those who are seen as running away from succession that are the best suited for leading the business in a new direction. The succession avoiders are the ones trying out new things, in many cases starting up new businesses, and it is this experimental activity that prepares them for a career of entrepreneurship. Not everything qualifies as entrepreneurship, of course, and not every next gen activity will ultimately contribute to the business. We can only advise current leaders to take a very broad view of what it takes to build a career that will one day enable a member of the next generation to take over.

If succession is to be for change, then entrepreneurial drive is more important than succession intention. In our view, the current generation of leaders should encourage the development of entrepreneurs in the next generation, over simple successors. This means being supportive, keeping an open mind, and not demanding to see relevance or results too quickly. Members of the next generation should be given reason to be interested in the core business of their own accord; obligation and a sense of responsibility are part of the deal in family and founder-led businesses and cannot be wished away, but they are not good bases for entrepreneurship and change.

6.2   Next Gen Groups

Singapore, one recent evening, in the multi-generation home of a local family business leader: eleven members of the next generation from seven family and founder-led businesses have convened to discuss the subject of preparing for succession with the author.[4] I present a couple of introductory ideas, and then the discussion begins. One young lady from Indonesia describes an internship in a bank that her father had arranged for her; another young lady talks about how her father has provided her and her brothers with nice offices, but given them only busywork to do; and a third focuses on how her relationship with her parents can get in the way of proving herself in the business. The question

---

[4] Most South East Asian family businesses are quite young, led by either the founder or the founder's immediate offspring. Thus, the members of the group described here are from the second generation.

on everybody's mind is how to gain meaningful experience at a young age. I probe their statements and different members of the group chip in with ideas and suggestions: the over thirties, in particular, offer concrete action steps. The spirit of the discussion is open and frank. They know each other and are used to sharing information and opinions on a wide variety of topics pertaining to their family businesses.

This Singapore-based group was founded by a couple of young men who wanted to create a forum where members of the next generation(s) could meet to exchange views and experiences in an informal, but stimulating setting. Meetings take place every few months, organized around topics of interest to the members: succession, diversification, entrepreneurship, philanthropy, to name just a few. Where possible, the group invites an external expert to kick off and facilitate the discussion. There are very few rules, not all members attend every session, and new members are invited. The group does not even have a name. The main conditions for membership, in addition to association with (but not necessarily full-time employment in) a family business of roughly comparable size, are interest and willingness to share.

While the loose structure and the spontaneous exchange that characterize the group faithfully reflect some of the characteristics of Generation Me described above (i.e. networked, open), these activities are not what one typically associates with family and founder led businesses. On the contrary, family and founder led businesses have a justified reputation for secrecy. In fact, some would say that secrecy is a key source of competitive advantage for these kinds of firms.[5] And yet, here we have the next generations of different firms, although none of them direct rivals, sitting around the same table exchanging views on questions that will ultimately affect the governance and the leadership of these firms. This represents an extraordinary, historical departure for family and founder-led businesses. The generational effect appears to be even stronger than the kinship effect. Or maybe the two effects coincide in this instance: as one of the founding members of the Singapore group said, "you can trust the members of family businesses to keep the content of what we discuss inside the group".

Note that the case of the self-organizing Singapore group is not unusual. Thus, to cite a few further examples: a group of interested Masters students organized the First London Business School Family Business Day in 2013 and continues to set up regular discussion days, allowing the next generations

---

[5] The tradition of secrecy is regularly alluded to in the literature on family firms and described as both an advantage and, in a few respects, as an impediment; cf. Stewart A, Hitt MA (2012) Why Can't a Family Business Be More Like a Nonfamily Business? Modes of Professionalization in Family Firms. Family Business Review, 25, 58–86.

of family and founder-led businesses to interact on questions of common interest; in the last couple of years, similar interest groups have sprung up at a number of other schools, in Europe, but also in North America and in Asia. Where no organized interest group exists, members of the next generation find each other: half of the respondents in a recent study of German family business children (defined as aged between nineteen and thirty-seven) reported talking to other individuals with similar backgrounds on a regular basis, with the objective of sharing both questions and answers.[6]

Not all of the networking and sharing among the next generations of family and founder-led businesses is self-organized. Firms involved in succession services (notably private banks and consultancies) and business schools also organize events focusing on knowledge exchange, for both the current and the next generations as well as purely for the next generation. These events are more formal than the self-organized groups and interactions, but the principles are the same: open exchange around topics of specific interest, frank discussion of issues, and networking, both between the succession service providers and the businesses, as well as *among* the representatives of the businesses. Sometimes, the providers even find themselves on the outside looking in, as conversations among interested individuals take on a dynamic of their own. Again, particularly at the level of the younger generation, the *within* business secrecy of old is superseded by the *among* business openness of today.

Unlike previous generations that did not look outside the inner circle for ideas, the next generation of today is not alone with its questions about succession in family and founder-led businesses. Of course, the current generation holds the key to the business, and members of the next generation are very conscious of this fact. All of the different forms of knowledge gathering and networking described here assist members of the next generation in making up their own minds about succession; just as importantly, however, these diverse external activities help them develop the confidence necessary to address issues with the current generation of leaders. Based on the exchanges with their peers in other family and founder-led businesses, the next generation has something substantial to say about what constitutes best practice in matters of succession, with multiple domestic and increasingly, international examples to draw upon. Not a few members of the current generation have found themselves surprised by the level of interest and expertise their potential successors display.

---

[6]Von Recklinghausen C (2012) Die Nachfolger von Familienunternehmen: Eine Betrachtung des Verhältnisses der jungen Generation zu ihrem Unternehmen, Bachelorarbeit, Alanus Hochschule, Alfter, Germany.

Going Against the Conventional Wisdom:

The next generation is self-centered and resists apprenticeship.—

In wanting to do its own thing, today's next generation is no different from past next generations. The criticisms of being self-centered and unwilling to learn from their elders are as old as humanity itself. Where today's next generation does differ from its predecessors is in its openness, both to trying new approaches and to communicating with others going through similar experiences. Moreover, in contrast to some past generations (think the youth of the 1960s and 1970s, for example), today's next generation is often deeply interested in business, not only as a means of making money, but also as a way of addressing social issues and moving the world forward. Openness, communication, and interest are great bases for actually succeeding in business, especially where the challenge is to innovate and find new ways of doing things. Rather than despairing of the next generation's supposed foibles, the current generation ought to take advantage of their predisposition to entrepreneurship.

Many, if not all members of the next generation have a deep interest in (the) business, but prefer to learn from and with their peers. The current generation can encourage this kind of learning and prepare the ground for succession discussions by engaging in an open exchange of ideas with their next gens. Again, it is important to realize that many of these ideas will not be of any immediate relevance to the core business. In fact, some of the discussions may never yield fruit for the core business. Still, the current generation should have an interest in this kind of exchange, both as a means of staying close to the next gens and as a way of accessing genuinely new approaches. After all, current leaders of family and founder-led businesses often belong to the "closed" generation, that is to say the generation that limited business discussions to the inner circle. Through the next generation, they, too, can benefit from the increasingly open exchange of ideas among businesses.

If openness is one of the defining characteristics of the next generation and openness is essential to innovation, then it is the job of current business leaders to find ways to take this spirit into the core business. Rather than only trying to teach, the current generation should also make an effort to learn. In a world that is changing at unprecedented speed, the current generation cannot expect to preserve old ways of thinking about the business. Even before succession is formally on the table, the current generation of leaders has a lot to learn from its potential successors.

6.3   Networks of Families

In business and especially so in family and founder-led businesses, the proof of the pudding is in doing, not talking. Quite naturally, some of the contacts made at the knowledge gathering and networking events lead to discussion of opportunities for doing business together. This is especially true in Asia, where firms are generally younger and more diversified and hence also more open to branching out into new lines of business that may not be related to the established core. Thus, examples like that of the son of a construction entrepreneur collaborating with the son of a finance entrepreneur on a new business to import rare vintages of Bordeaux into South East Asia are not uncommon and, what's more, do not seem that farfetched to the families involved. In Europe and the United States, examples such as this are relatively rare, but even in these more settled regions, the conversations of the next generation are not limited to questions of governance and family legacy, as individuals draw on each other for advice on how to start new business ventures, both within and outside the framework of the existing business. Members of the next generation find their counterparts in other family and founder led businesses to be excellent sparring partners and sometimes even business partners.

Cooperation between individuals from different families as a means of exploring new business opportunities may also be actively encouraged by the current generation of leaders in family and founder-led businesses. In several Asian examples, business families from different sectors have joined forces to work together on specific investment and development projects, as well as philanthropic endeavors. Like for the next generation exchanges, the structure supporting the idea is the loose network in which families and individuals participate on a case-by-case basis. Thus, members of the next generation of several leading Singapore-based business families are working together on an investment in a system of schools in China. Money provided by the parent's generation will not be enough for the investment to pay off—the next gens will have to actively manage the project over an extended period of time. From the point of the families concerned, the benefits of this kind of arrangement are two-fold: first, the next gens get hands on experience in a new venture, experience that will help prepare them for more responsibility down the line; less tangibly, but more profoundly, projects such as this cement ties between families. As one Singaporean entrepreneur put it, "the most valuable and enduring thing I can give my children isn't money or property, it's a network of trusted people to do business with".

Cooperation between individuals from different families and between different families represents a promising way to introduce succession for change. Unlike the traditional method of giving potential successors a protected playground for trying new ideas under the umbrella of the existing business, cooperation between families on new ventures exposes the next generation to disagreement and disconfirming evidence in a context of real world competition. Not all of these cooperative ventures work out, but very few unsuccessful ones are allowed to linger on just because they are a pet project of daddy's boy (or girl). With multiple funding sponsors to answer to and a broad variety of business experiences to draw upon, that is much less likely to happen.

<u>*Going Against the Conventional Wisdom*</u>:

The next generation should focus on learning the business from the inside.—

In general, inside experience is an important prerequisite for understanding the ins and outs, proving the candidate's mettle and eventually taking on the top job, especially in family and founder-led businesses. The critique of inside experience and indeed a career based on inside experience has always been focused on the question of perspective—without adequate outside experience, a leader risks missing or misunderstanding developments that occur outside the business, and, in a context of fleeting competitive advantage this is a fundamental risk. In family and founder-led businesses following the inside track also raises the question of favoritism—the offspring and cronies of the family or the founder are particularly vulnerable to this critique. Because the inside track is so fraught with danger, family and founder-led businesses have always tried to give potential successors a taste of the outside world, particularly in younger years, before they return to the fold of the core business. The possibility to run several businesses in partnership with other families challenges this dichotomy. In effect, it is now possible for members of the next generation to be active inside and outside at the same time.

The chance to run a new business in collaboration with peers from other family or founder-led businesses exposes potential successors to honest feedback under market conditions and helps them to hone a durable network of entrepreneurial contacts outside the firm. Just as importantly, it allows potential successors to build a career inside the core business while maintaining an external perspective that is subject to continuous validation. Inside and outside together—there can be no better preparation for succession, especially succession for change that relies on internal knowledge and external perspective.

The current generation of people at the top of family and founder-led businesses would do well to encourage potential successors in the running of new businesses in collaboration with peers, but they have to be careful to resist the impulse to get involved beyond seed funding. It is critical that the next generation has the freedom to do it their way, to prove their ability in their own space and on their own terms. Once they have created the conditions for founding new businesses, current leaders should sit back and watch. Peer interaction and market opinion will make or break these new businesses and provide vital data on the aptitude of potential successors.

6.4 Conclusion

In many cases, the next generation is preparing itself very well for succession for change. Most critically and quite novel from the point of view of their elders, members of the next generation are taking their careers and therefore also the question of succession into their own hands. Working across families, in whatever form, gives the next gens the opportunity to experience the world as it exists outside of the cocoon of the family or founder-led business.

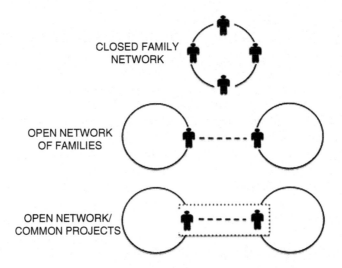

CLOSED FAMILY
NETWORK

OPEN NETWORK
OF FAMILIES

OPEN NETWORK/
COMMON PROJECTS

Fig. 6.1   The next generation: from closed and isolated to open and linked

This leads to new ideas and concrete new opportunities. For many next gens, the old inside outside career dichotomy—inside the family business or outside the family business—does not hold anymore. They might work inside the family business and pursue projects outside the family business; or, they might work outside the family business, but stay connected to the family business via family business conferences. As a result, they see more, ask more challenging questions of the family business, and are more change ready.

Of course, not all potential successors in family and founder-led businesses are as open and as entrepreneurial as the ones described here. Indeed, as the Ernst Young/University of St. Gallen survey cited earlier implies, the more entrepreneurial among the next generation may be less likely to want to succeed to the top of their predecessor's firm, preferring to make their own way in a firm that they have founded themselves. The challenge then is to ensure that the entrepreneurial, networked individual(s) and their projects remain relevant to the established business, because given their openness and bias for action, they are eminently suited to play a major role in succession for change. In effect, they may combine some of the best characteristics of both internal and external candidates for succession: deep knowledge of the firm and the established business and deep knowledge of how to create a viable business outside the firm.

In working with the next generation, one has to recognize that succession for change is as much about developing the business as about preparing the leadership transition. With new business (and governance) ideas emerging frequently from the probing and experimenting of the next generation, the current generation needs to build in ways to try and test, not just the person, but also the ideas. Some will succeed, some will fail, but in the process the core business itself will benefit and become better prepared for change. Encouraging entrepreneurial behavior in the next generation and loosely tying the results of this entrepreneurship to the future of the core business can help set the stage for succession for change. The important thing to keep in mind is that the next generation, with ideas and with achievements based on the tests of the world outside the family or founder-led business, will play a big role in shaping the succession process. Those who are ultimately capable of leading succession for change will not sit back and expect succession to just come to them (Fig. 6.1).

Part III

Perspectives

The concluding chapters assess the futures of family and founder-led businesses, present a framework for implementing succession as transformation, and rethink succession governance. We show that when change becomes the focus of succession, building on entrepreneurial values takes precedence over preserving the status quo; succession planning evolves from an episodic to a continuous process; and the emphasis of succession governance shifts from executive selection to strategic direction.

7

Succession in a World of Change

Timing. As a way of addressing the problem of synchronicity, the gap in time between when strategic change is needed and when a leader is "naturally" ready to move on, we introduce the idea of succession as a continuous process and suggest ways to implement the idea in practice.

Values. In order to be ready for change, family and founder-led businesses need to find a way to bottle the entrepreneurial spirit that got the firm off the ground in the first place. By encouraging and rewarding those individuals who make change their mission, entrepreneurial values contribute to building a pool of potential successors who have skill in creating something new.

Future(s). Family and founder-led businesses traditionally source successors in leadership from a narrow group of individuals. A loose partnership of families or firms gives access to a broader, more diverse pool of leaders that a family or founder-led business can tap as needed, for the firm as a whole, or for part of the firm, with the possibility of splitting off the part that comes under new leadership.

The last twenty-five years have seen an unprecedented amount of upheaval in business. Many developing economies have joined the ranks of the developed economies; many industries of long standing have altered beyond recognition; and many famous old corporations have been absorbed or gone bankrupt. The impermanence of competitive advantage has had a significant impact on succession in family and founder-led businesses, leading to an increase in exits and founder returns, as well as new ways of preparing both outsiders and insiders for leadership. Succession services, in turn, have been evolving from an almost exclusive emphasis on succession for continuity to a more balanced

© The Author(s) 2017
H. Korine, *Succession for Change*, DOI 10.1007/978-3-319-52120-6_7

view that starts with an analysis of the business and includes succession for change as a real alternative. Open to new ideas and connected beyond the confines of the firm, the next generation of leaders is generally well aware of the impermanence of competitive advantage and actively looking for ways to drive change. As pointed out in the early chapters, succession has always been defined by the objective of continuity. What does the succession process look like when change is the focus?

In order to understand the succession process today and going forward, it is important not only to examine what is different today, but also to recognize what is still the same in the choreography of current generation leaders, advisors, and next generation successors in family and founder-led businesses, as they individually and jointly try to cope with the impermanence of competitive advantage. First of all, at the strategic level, the impermanence of competitive advantage has not eliminated or reduced organizational inertia. Broad strategic change is still difficult to commit to and implement, especially in businesses that bear the strong imprint of a single family or individual. However, in today's context of short-lived competitive advantage, decisive choice is more important than ever: simply riding out the storm is not an option, when the storm can destroy the basis of the business. Analogously, at the level of the current leadership, emotional attachment to the business and, in many cases, to existing strategies and practices can be a block to resolute action. Bold steps like exit or choosing a successor who embodies change are likely to clash with the current leaders' attachment to the status quo. Advisors are also conflicted between what has not changed and what is different today. They know that the economic context requires a focus on the future of the business and a willingness to work for change, but they also recognize that advocating change and more particularly succession for change risks alienating current leaders who prefer the established way of doing things. The next generation, finally, probably sees the conflict between present and future more clearly than anyone; they are hardwired to be open to going new ways, but they are also "soft-wired" from childhood to be aware of the legacy concerns of their elders and would like to satisfy these wherever possible. In sum, what is different today and driving succession for change faces stiff resistance from what is still the same and would encourage succession for continuity. Table 7.1 presents a juxtaposition of what is different and what is the same at the levels discussed in this book (with chapter numbers in parenthesis).

Our analysis suggests that managing succession for change is as much about dealing with the forces for continuity as it is about responding to the drivers of change. Organizational inertia, emotional attachment to the status quo, advisor reticence to rock the boat, and concern for family or founder legacy,

Table 7.1 Succession today: what is different? What is the same?

	What is different? (drivers of change)	What is the same? (forces for continuity)
Strategy (3)	Importance of decisive choices	Organizational inertia
Family/founder (4)	Need for resolute action	Attachment to status quo; concern for legacy
Advisors (5)	Focus on the future of the business	Reticence to advocate change
Next gen (6)	Openness to going new ways	Concern for family/founder legacy

characteristics especially pronounced in family and founder-led businesses that have been built on the long-term commitment of a single family or individual, do not disappear in the brave new world of impermanent competitive advantage. Instead, these characteristics combine to make succession for change more difficult. At every level and for every category of actor we describe, succession for change poses a dilemma: how to advance change without getting stymied by organizational and psychological realities on the ground.

In this chapter, we explore the relationship between succession for change and the forces for continuity in family and founder-led businesses. Whereas previous chapters were built upon reviews of extant literature, hard data, and case histories, this chapter is more speculative in nature. Reflecting upon the role that succession can play both in supporting continuity and encouraging change leads us to question the episodic timing of succession; we propose rethinking succession as a continuous process. Reconsidering the forces for continuity and the drivers of change in succession motivates the development of an alternative point of view of what is to be transmitted in the transition from one generation of leadership to the next; we suggest that efforts to maintain the family/founder culture be refocused on establishing and perpetuating entrepreneurial values. This leads to a new point of departure for thinking about the futures of family and founder-led businesses.

7.1   Timing

The conflict between drivers of change and forces for continuity is not unique to succession, but the issues tend to crystallize around succession. In many handbooks on change, decisive choice, resolute action, and openness to new ways are contrasted with organizational inertia, emotional attachment to the status quo, and concern for family or founder legacy (the role of advisors is mentioned only rarely); the event of succession marks the time when the rubber meets the road, and conflict which is latent comes out in to the open. As continuity is often seen as a defining and desirable characteristic of businesses identified with a family or a founder, succession is one of the rare instances when it is considered legitimate to discuss the conflict between change and continuity in these kinds of businesses. With successions few and far between, these represent critical opportunities to analyze and possibly reorient the business.

Despite the focus on change in this book, it is important to recognize that the forces for continuity also play a positive role in business performance. Without the investment in perfecting processes that engenders organizational inertia and without the commitment to a specific approach that creates emotional attachment, no business can survive the rigors of competition. Just as we do not wish to glorify change, we do not wish to malign continuity. What is required in a world of impermanent competitive advantage is the ability to find a balance between change and continuity, not to let the forces for continuity to prevent all change, nor to let the drivers of change make any kind of continuity impossible. Without such a balance, the only way the system as a whole can evolve is by violent rupture, recalling the fights and even wars associated with succession for change in history and literature. Succession has a pivotal position in the conflict between the drivers of change and the forces for continuity, as a change in leadership invariably puts the question of change versus continuity on the table. In our view, one of the essential problems in family and founder-led businesses is that of *synchronicity*. Only in rare cases does the "natural" timing of succession—when the leader in office is ready to depart—felicitously match the appropriate timing for instigating a business change.

The tenure of the typical leader of a successful family or founder-led business is long: twenty or even thirty years at the top are not uncommon. Again, constancy in leadership and strategy is often seen as one of the roots of success of these businesses. However, such long periods of leadership also strengthen the forces for continuity, allowing processes to turn into rigidities, commitments to a way of doing business to become unshakable emotional attachments, relationships with advisors to harden into interdependencies, and legacy concerns to override economic rationality. In these circumstances, the episode of succession carries undue weight, in effect an all or nothing, once in a generation chance to alter the course of the business. Of course, some leaders are able to pay careful attention to the drivers of change and balance the conflicting needs of continuity and change over a long period of time. Succession is not the only window of opportunity for addressing these questions. Still, the episodic timing of succession, particularly in family and founder-led businesses, tends to reinforce and dramatize the conflict between continuity and change.

What if succession were rethought as a continuous, rather than a periodic process? Interestingly, a very old and in other ways quite traditional family business, the Geneva private bank Pictet & Cie., established in 1805, provides an example of what a continuous succession process can look like in practice. Pictet is run by a group of seven to nine equally powerful managing partners who are also the sole owners of the business. It is a family business, because at least two of the partners must come from the Pictet family, but it is a family business with a twist, because the other partners almost always come from a group of unrelated, Geneva based families. In effect, Pictet is a multi-family family business in which only the managing partners have an ownership interest. What makes Pictet so interesting, from the point of view of succession, is that the managing partners range in age from forty to sixty—retirements and new entries occur in parallel. In this way, the succession discussion never stops.[1]

The ongoing discussion about succession allows the bank to match emerging needs with the requisite skills at the top. Thus, in the last fifteen years, for example, new partners have brought new strengths in asset management, emerging markets, and technology to a leadership team that had in the past been more narrowly focused on the bank's traditional mainstay in private banking for European clients. Every partner still has to have a generalist's ability to comprehend the entire range of businesses, but the continuous addition of diverse expertise at the top has allowed the bank to act upon emerging trends of significance in a gradual way, without major stops and starts. Put simply, the shorter cycle of succession practiced by Pictet is better suited to an industry in flux than the once in a generation model of succession common in family and founder led businesses. Maintaining a multi-generation team of partners allows the bank to combine the best of continuity and change in succession.

A retired partner, Ivan Pictet, told me that he does not believe that the bank's model of succession can be applied 'tel quel' (as is) to other family firms—dependent as it is on the shared values of a particular community of families that have grown together over several centuries.[2] This does not mean that the Pictet model of continuous succession has no general insights to offer. Indeed not a few professional service firms organize succession along similar lines, continuously renewing the leadership by introducing new partners on a periodic basis, albeit not at the very top like Pictet and generally without any family connection. What might a continuous succession process à la Pictet look like in more traditionally structured family and founder-led businesses?

---

[1] The Pictet process of succession is described in considerable detail by Simon FB, Wimmer R., and Groth T (2005) Das Pictet-Modell. In: Mehr-Generationen-Familienunternehmen: Erfolgsgeheimnisse, von Oetker, C&A, u.a., Carl Auer Verlag, Heidleberg.

[2] Personal interview with Ivan Pictet, Geneva, February 26, 2015.

First of all, the notion of a continuous succession process suggests the need for continuous dialogue among decision-makers and among generations. Rather than thinking about succession in an episodic manner, that is to say when the need arises, or, even more rarely, in the event of leader incapacity, succession could become a recurring topic, to be seriously considered in the same rhythm as strategy, or on an annual basis. For a leader who is at the beginning of his/her tenure or if possible successors are still very young, this may seem unrealistic; however, the idea to better synchronize succession and strategy is born out of a very real need to be proactive. In a context of impermanent competitive advantage, it is never too early to talk about succession. The content of such discussions will vary with the personal situations of leaders and successors and the economic environment of the business. For a succession conversation to maintain meaning over a longer period of time, it is important to avoid routine—just another topic on the agenda—and adjust to changing conditions. The business evolves, and so should the discussion about succession.

Beyond the discussion about succession, a continuous process à la Pictet also implies sharing leadership responsibilities, particularly where new fields of business are concerned. The obvious thing to do is to strive for a generational mix across businesses and functions, with younger leaders given the chance to prove themselves in emerging technologies and markets, where their youth is an advantage (see also Chap. 4, on the grooming of insiders). The danger in sticking rigorously to this rule is that it prevents the younger generation from gaining experience in leading the established businesses, a shortcoming that will damage their credibility when the time comes for succession to actually take place. One cannot expect the coach of the junior farm team to take over the first team without the requisite know-how. The solution is to ensure that potential successors build bridges from the new fields to the established businesses: this prepares the established businesses for change and forces potential successors to make their case(s) for change to those parts of the organization that are least predisposed to change.

Going Against the Conventional Wisdom:
  Succession is an episodic process, to be launched on a generational basis.—
  Succession as an episodic process works fine in a world of sustainable competitive advantage. When major technological or regulatory changes come along once every generation or even less frequently, the timing of episodic successions as they have been common in family and founder-led businesses, say once every twenty or thirty years, is likely to match or closely approximate the timing of significant strategic adaptations. In a world of much more frequent change, where competitive advantage can be won

and lost in a few years, succession needs to be thought about as a continuous process. In the same way as strategy has to be continuously adjusted in light of rapidly chang- ing competitive parameters, discussion about and implementation of succession should be ongoing. The same leader may be able to navigate multiple competitive shifts, but the succession process has to keep up with the strategy process.

The two most evident arguments against succession as a continuous process are instability at the top and disruption in the organization. If succession is always on the table, then leadership will feel threatened, and employees will be exposed to unnecessary uncertainty. These arguments can best be countered by making the suc- cession process part of business as usual for boards and directors. In this way, the succession process becomes an integral part of the leadership agenda and loses some of the drama typically associated with it. If leaders are used to discussing succession as part of their review of strategy, and if employees are made aware that succession is an ongoing process, not an episodic process, then succession for change will cause less upheaval. Just like at Pictet, leaders and employees will come to expect continuous consideration of change at the top as normal.

The point here is not to imply that leadership change needs to happen all the time: the kind of stop and start leadership with extremely short CEO tenures practiced in many listed companies is not conducive to successful strategic adaptation. Rather, it is a symbol of panic in the face of change and an inadequate, episodic succession process. Making the process of succession continuous, on the other hand, works against panic and prepares the leadership and the organization for choosing the right people at the right time.

Not all, in fact very few family and founder-led businesses have the talent necessary to run the firm over generations in the family or in-house. Here again, the example of Pictet provides suggestive ideas. Based on the evidence that Pictet draws its successors in ownership both from the Pictet family and from a group of unrelated, Geneva-based families, we called the firm a multi-family family business. The question is whether and how this concept might also be applied, in some form, to family and founder-led businesses that have traditionally had one base of ownership. In fact, families and founder-led busi- nesses are already cooperating in a number of ways: the multi-family office exists to service the financial and investment needs of a group of families, each of which, in isolation, is too small to be able to afford such a service; family and founder-led businesses also support each other on specific transactions, such as Warren Buffett's loan to Mars, Inc. in the latter's 2008 purchase of Wrigley. Most relevant, from the point of view adopted here, are the examples of South East Asian family businesses investing together for the purpose of developing ties among the next generation cited in Chap. 6. From the practice of invest- ing together for developing ties to some form of multi-family family business the distance is not insurmountable. At least a part of each original firm could come under this heading, with the possibility of growing into something that is independent of the parent firms and providing the potential for a pool of successors from outside the ownership group of the legacy business.

As a way of addressing the problem of synchronicity, the gap in time between when strategic change is needed and when a leader is "naturally" ready to move on, we introduced the idea of succession as a continuous process and drew on the example of Pictet to suggest ways to implement the idea in practice. Succession as a continuous process involves encouraging constructive dialogue, sharing leadership responsibilities, and, in some cases at least, cooperating with other family and founder-led businesses in the development of new businesses and leadership talent. In other words, succession as a continuous process sows the seeds for change. Central to any discussion about succession and critical when succession involves change is the consideration of values: what are the values that have made the firm successful, and what are the values that will allow the firm to successfully adapt as the world around it evolves?

7.2   Values

The business may change, but the values of the family and the founder endure—this is one of the mantras of family and founder-led businesses, and, as we discussed in Chap. 1, leaders and advisors spend a lot of time spelling out what these values are. Not surprisingly, given its importance for the future of the business, a discussion about succession often serves as a launching point for articulating family or founder values and putting them into writing. If succession is more about change than continuity, and if the process is continuous rather than episodic, then the Ten Commandments image of setting down the definite values of the firm needs to be revised. For change to be possible, values have to be alive and relevant to leading change.

At the start-up stage, a business is almost infinitely flexible and responsive. With growth and success come structure and processes intended to ensure efficient replication. The firm becomes "good" at what it does. Codifying what makes the firm special is meant to guarantee ongoing success and cement the family's or the founder's legacy. Even if the leaders step down or move on, important decisions will still be taken with their values in mind. Mars, Inc., a well-known and enduring success story among family businesses, provides a representative example of the kinds of values we are talking about. In 1983, at the time of the final leadership transition from the second to the third generation and some seventy years into the history of the firm, Mars articulated and published a set of five values (called Principles): quality, responsibility, mutuality, efficiency, and freedom.[3] Since then, the Five Principles have been updated twice (in 1993 and in 2003), with changes in emphasis, but not in substance. By all accounts, they are well accepted in the firm and continue to have a strong influence on strategic decisions.

A set of values like the Five Principles of Mars provide guidance about what to do and what not to do. Thus, the principle of freedom, for example, holds that the firm should not take on risks that may force it to go into excessive debt or to share ownership outside the family; this means that the firm always has to make enough profit to finance its growth ambitions. The principles of quality and efficiency, taken together, imply that the firm should not go into businesses that it does not master and cannot make a reasonable return from. Over the years, adherence to the Five Principles has largely protected the firm from missteps and ensured that it continues to improve on what it does best, that is to say producing and marketing fast moving consumer goods. Many family businesses that make it to the third generation have similar values and have done very well by sticking to them. As stated earlier, family businesses often define themselves by continuity, and strong values are a critical element of living continuity. The question is what happens when continuity is not appropriate. What kinds of values can help to drive change?

Every business is originally based on an entrepreneurial insight and on entrepreneurial behavior, and the values underlying this kind of insight and behavior are precisely what change requires. In order to be ready for change, family and founder-led businesses need to find a way to bottle the entrepreneurial spirit that got the firm off the ground in the first place. Beyond the genius of the founder, the entrepreneurial spirit is embodied in a very specific attitude towards markets and resources. Entrepreneurs generally do not target existing markets, nor do they base their approach on accumulated resources; instead, entrepreneurs look for new markets at the interstices of existing markets and recombine resources from all over. New market discovery and resource recombination are the watchwords of entrepreneurship.

Could the watchwords of entrepreneurship also function as values for sustaining a successful family or founder-led business in transition from one generation of leadership to the next? Recasting new market discovery and resource recombination as values would yield statements along the following lines:

---

[3] www.mars.com/global/assets/documents/433657mars_the_five_principles_of_mars_without_signatures_V2.pdf.

(a) We continuously and patiently seek out new markets, invest in a variety of new opportunities and reward people for finding new market space; we will not be caught out by new types of demand or new technologies.

(b) We make use of resources from all over, strive to maintain the highest level of knowledge about what resources are available and how they can be tapped; we will not fall not victim to the not-invented-here syndrome.

Interestingly, entrepreneurial values of the kind articulated above are rarely found in company value statements, whether the business is family or founder led.[4] Whereas we are advocating values related to what has been called the process of creative destruction, most value statements enshrine values that have to do with maintaining the status quo. If succession is to be about readying the organization for change, then the values developed in the course of the succession process have to reflect that. Again, some degree of continuity is always desirable in organizations. The important thing is not to create a mismatch between succession and values: succession for change can only build on values for change.

Entrepreneurial values such as the ones outlined above support and reinforce a continuous process of succession. By encouraging and rewarding those individuals who make change their mission, entrepreneurial values contribute to building a pool of potential successors who have skill in creating something new. In this way, succession is experienced by the organization as less of a rupture and more of a gradual transition. When the new businesses have blossomed, their leader(s) will be ready to take on greater responsibility for the whole. In part, succession takes place before the current leadership actually steps down.

Going Against the Conventional Wisdom:
Corporate values define what stays the same over time.—
The first step to flexibility in family and founder-led businesses is accepting that the business is unlikely to look the same as it does today in twenty, ten, or even five years from now. The people at the top, especially if they are nearing the end of their careers, need to understand that the best legacy they can leave is a focus on keeping the business ready for change. If, Rip van Winkle-like, they were one day to return after a long absence, the business would not look anything like what they left behind, but it would still exist and still be driven by the values for change that the outgoing leaders

---

[4] For an interesting exception to this general rule and an example supporting the argument advanced here, see the description of how entrepreneurial values are embraced as both business values and family values in the Singapore-based Korvac Holdings, in Kralik M, Glemser AC (2014) "Korvac Holdings: What Makes a Family Business", IMD Case, IMD-7-1502.

inspired. In other words, corporate values can just as well define what needs to change as what needs to stay the same. By going back to the watchwords for entrepreneurship—new market discovery and resource recombination—leaders can develop values for change that provide essential support to succession for change.

Does this mean that values for continuity can be dispensed with entirely? Clearly, values for continuity also fulfill an important function, namely to provide guidelines that preserve the essence of what makes the organization different from others. The point, then, is not to eliminate traditional value statements, but to recognize the limitations they impose and complement them with values for change. The effort to preserve what exists often obscures the entrepreneurship that created and grew the business; values for change make entrepreneurship central again. In thinking about strategy and considering succession in times of continuous competitive challenge, values for change are the essential guidelines that will enable leaders to wholeheartedly embrace a new direction—in the spirit of those who went before them.

New market discovery and resource recombination are the basic ingredients of any kind of entrepreneurship. For each family and founder-led business, these ingredients will have their own specific flavors, influenced by the personalities of the leaders and the history of the organization. Each business needs to define for itself the roles of customer definition and technology competence in their values for change. Ultimately, values for change have to be faithful to the business, inspirational and actionable.

7.3 Future(s) of Family and Founder-Led Businesses

In a very real sense, this is the age of family and founder-led businesses: as a group, family businesses have done very will to survive the economic turmoil that followed the collapse of the US housing market and the subsequent great recession; founder-led businesses and, more particularly, start-ups have been at the forefront of bringing new business models to many established industries. Why then, do we worry about navigating succession for change and want to talk about the future(s) of family and founder-led businesses? The present seems like such a good place to be.

First of all, we should not let the present good times obscure the longer term challenges posed by the impermanence of competitive advantage. While it is true that many family businesses have weathered the recent storms better than their listed counterparts, that does not mean that the problem of succession for change has gone away; on the contrary, the success of so many start-ups with new business models makes the problem more relevant than ever. Second, the basic questions raised in this chapter about the timing of succession and the values transmitted in succession require us to rethink what family and founder-led businesses might look like if succession for change becomes the norm and some of the novel ideas discussed here are more widely adopted.

Family and founder-led businesses have traditionally been defined by the personality and character of the people who have given their name to the firm. Even long after the founder has retired or passed on, family and founder-led businesses have maintained the values of the people who shaped their formative years. Continuity has been the virtue that separates these businesses from those listed companies that follow fashion and bend in the wind.[5] The emphasis on continuity and the emotional attachment to strategies and values that have become identified with individuals who have played decisive historical roles are what make succession for change so difficult for family and founder-led businesses. If these businesses are to become proficient at adapting to the impermanence of competitive advantage, then they will have to transform. Succession will need to be conceived of as a continuous, rather than an episodic process and entrepreneurial values will have to take precedence over values formulated to limit risk and preserve the status quo. These changes, in turn, have the potential to reshape the nature of leadership and alter the ownership structure of family and founder-led firms.

Single person leadership increases the weight of the succession decision and makes errors especially costly. In a context of repeated change, it may therefore be advisable to give serious consideration to a multi-headed model of leadership. Not only does a multi-headed model à la Pictet reduce the pressure to find the one right successor, it also provides a leadership pool for the firm to draw upon. When new developments are coming at the firm from many directions, a diverse leadership pool with experience in a variety of entrepreneurial ventures inside and outside the firm may be better suited for comprehending and implementing change involving new market discovery and resource recombination. Of course, the notion of a leadership pool goes against the founder or CEO as hero model of leadership that many firms and many observers adhere to. And yet, many family businesses have been started and run by siblings, and most founder-led businesses have depended upon a core team of associates surrounding the founder. Some form of multi-headed model of leadership with a chief who is primus inter pares (first among equals) would be a better representation of entrepreneurial values than the traditional single person model and make continuous succession easier to institutionalize.[6]

Family and founder-led businesses traditionally source successors in leadership from a narrow group of individuals—family members or close colleagues

---

[5] For a discussion of the forces pressuring listed companies to follow fashion, see Alexander M, Korine H (2008) When you shouldn't go global. Harvard Business Review, December.

[6] The conditions under which shared leadership arrangements can be viable are discussed in Lansberg I (1999) Succeeding Generations. Harvard Business School Press, Cambridge, MA (see Chapter 5).

of the founder. The proposed multi-headed model of leadership requires a more diverse pool of leaders than these businesses typically possess. The question is whether all of the leaders have to reside in the same firm. In a multi-family family firm or in an association of family/founder firms, the problem of adequate leadership reserves is solved in a different way. Essentially, a loose partnership of families or firms gives access to a broader, more diverse pool of leaders that a family or founder-led business can tap as needed, for the firm as a whole, or for part of the firm, with the possibility of splitting off the part that comes under new leadership, perhaps as a joint venture between two or more firms. For the current generation of leadership a partnership of firms may be difficult to imagine let alone put in to action, but the next generation of leaders is particularly adept at seeking advice and cooperation from outside the firm. This predisposition of the next generation would seem to favor the alternative approach to ownership described here.

> *Going Against the Conventional Wisdom*:
> *Single person leadership is the only way to go.—*
> *In family and founder-led businesses, the departure of the senior family leader or the founder leaves very large shoes to fill. In many cases, the reputation of the departing leader is such that no successor can possibly hope to do as well, no matter what the economic context. In other words, successors of larger than life leaders may be set up to fail. Here, the sacrosanct principle of unity of command conflicts with the very real difficulty of replacing a heroic leadership figure, and, if the succession doesn't work out as expected and the business flounders, doubters will be quick to undermine the new leader. If the previous leader is still available, he or she may be called into action again or indeed take the reins of his or her own accord. As the data in Chap. 4 show, competitive instability makes this course of action even more likely, especially if the successor was put in place to ensure continuity.*
> *With the impermanence of competitive advantage also comes a need to think about leadership in a more holistic manner, with consideration of multiple heads and from diverse sources. Especially for larger, more complex firms, revisiting the question in this way offers new models for organizing the succession process. Instead focusing on finding the one person capable of following the great leader—in many cases an impossible task—and thereby putting all of the metaphorical eggs in one basket, allowing for multiple leaders gives the business a broader base from which to navigate change, and, if necessary, eventually choosing the one leader who is capable of taking the firm forward. Going from one leader to multiple leaders also cushions the shock of losing the driving force behind the business and gives successors more time to prove themselves.*
> *Family and founder-led businesses are notorious for having a narrower leadership gene pool than other types of firms. No matter what the other strengths of the business, the combination of a narrow leadership gene pool and single leader succession is*

dangerous, particularly so in a context of continuous competitive challenge. It doesn't have to be that way, and some businesses are actively experimenting with alternatives to the traditional model.

The idea of family and founder-led businesses working together to adapt and change with the times recalls dynastic families of earlier eras who intermarried to grow their domains and consolidate control over large parts of society. In today's world of impermanent competitive advantage, cooperation among families and businesses has to be much more dynamic. In keeping with the speculative nature of this chapter, we can imagine businesses from around the world cooperating on an as needs basis, not only to address particular market needs, but also to develop a portfolio of entrepreneurial ventures and a deep pool of potential successors. Evidence presented in Chap. 6 suggests that some family and founder-led businesses and their next generation leaders are already taking tentative steps in this direction.

7.4   Conclusion

This chapter explored the relationship between succession for change and the drivers of continuity in family and founder-led businesses. Reflecting upon the role that succession can play both in supporting continuity and encouraging change led us to question the episodic timing of succession and to propose rethinking succession as a continuous process. Reconsidering the drivers of continuity and change in succession motivated the development of an alternative point of view of what can be transmitted in the transition from one generation of leadership to the next: we suggested that efforts to maintain the family/founder culture be refocused on establishing and perpetuating the entrepreneurial values that originally created the basis for a successful business and can serve as touch points for transformation, both today and in the future. Building on the concepts of continuous succession and entrepreneurial values, finally, we discussed the possibilities of a multi-headed model of leadership and a multi-family model of the family firm.

Succession for change implies more uncertainty and more conflict than succession for continuity, uncertainty about the right way forward and conflict about the right person to entrust with the power to transform the business. It is certainly no accident that succession for change has historically been associated with disorder and war. To the question 'is succession for change manageable?' the answer can only be 'not by the same methods as succession for continuity'. Designating the best person or people for the job is still

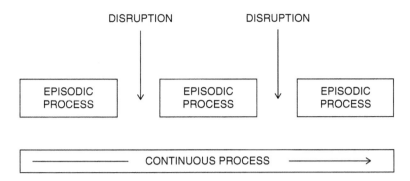

Fig. 7.1   The succession process: episodic vs. continuous

paramount, but not as an episode of succession planning, divorced from the broader changes affecting the business and the organization. In the last two chapters, we will draw out the implications of succession for change for strategy and governance, describing a comprehensive approach to transformation and defining the roles to be played by current leaders, owners, boards of directors, and advisors (Fig. 7.1).

8

Succession as Transformation

Succession … and Strategy. Succession for change has far-reaching implications for strategy and hence also for organization and ownership. These implications need to be taken into account when considering succession for change.

Succession … and Power. One of the most important things decision makers can do is to take the concerns of stakeholders seriously and to include a wide variety of voices in the strategy cum succession process.

Advice for Advisors. Not only do advisors need to have a deep understanding of the business they are consulting to and be able to offer a full range of services, from leadership selection to governance, they also have to become experts at change management and be willing to work closely with their clients on implementing succession for change.

Succession for change is never just about succession. We have already examined the financial, legal, and psychological aspects of succession in family and founder-led businesses and pointed out how these are affected by a focus on change. What we have not yet explored in detail are the *consequences* of succession for change. Unlike succession for continuity, succession for change has a decisive impact on the strategy of a firm; a redirection of strategy, in turn, necessarily leads to changes in organization and, at least in those cases where it is tradable, in ownership, as some shareholders rally around the new strategy, while others refuse to support it.[1] In line with its effect on the strategy, succession

---

[1] The notion that different strategic challenges call for different types of successors is discussed in Lansberg I (1999) Succeeding Generations.

© The Author(s) 2017
H. Korine, *Succession for Change*, DOI 10.1007/978-3-319-52120-6_8

for change engenders winners and losers and thereby also alters the balance of power in a firm. A new balance of power can have important implications for the aspirations of individuals and decisively influence corporate governance. Given the stakes, for the strategy and for the balance of power, it is no surprise that the implementation of succession for change is almost always subject to intense negotiation and, not infrequently, dramatic conflict among stakeholders.

In this chapter, we address the consequences of succession for change and adopt a normative approach to assist decision makers in thinking through and implementing the intended transformation. The key idea to keep in mind is that succession for change represents an entrepreneurial choice. In other words, we are talking not only about the selection of a person (or people) to lead the business, but also about a choice of markets and resources. As such, succession for change has an impact on all facets of the business, far beyond the person of the leader. As discussed in Chap. 4, thinking seriously about succession for change may even result in a sale of the business. When succession for change is on the table, every question is legitimate. Decision-makers need to be aware of the potential consequences of succession for change and be prepared to address them, as the succession process unfolds.

8.1   Succession and … Strategy

At this point, it is important to recall that the purpose of succession for change is to make a change of strategy happen. The reasoning behind succession for change is that a change of leadership will facilitate a change of strategy. A change of leadership can never be the whole story in implementing a change of strategy, but, particularly in family and founder-led businesses, where the conservative influence of the family or the founder can be very strong, succession and the legitimacy it confers are especially important elements of strategic transformation.

In contrast to most publicly listed companies, family and founder-led businesses typically do not have powerful outside shareholders or strong independent directors to help them recognize when strategic change is imperative or indeed to push them to make a strategic change. In effect, decision-makers in family and founder-led businesses are responsible for their own succession. In many cases, it is the leader himself/herself who needs to come to the realization that the business needs a different strategic emphasis and new skills at the top.

If the timing of succession for change is to be right, then the leadership in place needs to recognize the need for change early enough to prepare. As discussed in Chap. 7, the cycle of succession in family and founder-led businesses is typically much longer than in publicly listed firms, and the need for change is therefore highly unlikely to coincide with the date when the leader in place is "naturally" ready to retire. Quite on the contrary, increasingly short periods of competitive advantage pose an unprecedented challenge to all but the most adaptable leaders and founders.

Chapter 3 described the economic transformation of the last twenty-five years and explained the forces behind the disappearance of sustained competitive advantage. Most striking in this account were the extent of changes across industries and the pace of technological advances. As these developments continue, the leaders of family and founder-led businesses who are responsible for their own succession face the twin but related difficulties of understanding industry evolution and accepting that they may not be the right people to take the business into the next round. This is a very tall order for anyone, but especially trying for individuals who are likely to have an emotional attachment both to the business and to the way it is run.

This is why it is important that discussions about strategy and succession go hand in hand. Not every threat or opportunity need or should entail a transformative response: some developments are better addressed by a look-see approach while others don't require any action at all. However, only if it is conducted at the highest level, supported by rich data, will a strategy discussion yield the kind of insight about the future state of competition necessary for making the entrepreneurial choice of succession for change. In other words, it is advisable to make sure that strategy conversations have enough depth and are given sufficient standing to be able to consider emerging needs for new leadership.

Going Against the Conventional Wisdom:
   Strategy and succession are separate items on the agenda.—
   In the context of impermanent competitive advantage, every strategy discussion entails thinking about change and the leadership skills necessary to make that change happen. Thinking about strategy means thinking about the future of the business, not only about current customers, but also about currently untapped customers, not only about technologies in use, but also about up-and-coming technologies, and not only about existing competitors, but also about potential competitors from beyond the industry as defined today. When these kinds of questions are raised, leadership is confronted with its own limitations. Even to understand the potential futures of the business, let alone to navigate them successfully, it is necessary to gain a working knowledge of all of these developments. Some leaders will be able to adapt and learn how to take the business into the future, but not all.

In start-ups, it is common to reflect on whether the leader who brought the busi-ness so far is also the person to take business to the next stage. The leadership skills required for a start-up are different from the leadership skills needed to run an estab-lished business. New customers, new technologies and new competitors, or some com-bination thereof, are just as unsettling to a business as the transition from start-up to established business. Nonetheless, in established businesses that are on a defined tra-jectory it is much less common to think about whether the current leadership has the skills to take the business into the next phase of its life. In our view, if a thorough strategic analysis shows that an established business needs to reinvent itself, then the leadership should also ask itself, just like the start-up CEO and board ask themselves, do we have the right skills to take the business to the next level?

Considering strategy and succession side by side allows decision makers to opti-mally prepare the business for change. Preparing the business for change imperatively requires thinking about the leadership capabilities required to move the business forward and establish it in a new context. In addition to understanding new custom-ers, new technologies, and new competitors, the person at the top has to be able and willing to make required changes and, eventually, lead a very different business. The succession question follows naturally from this kind of reflection. Much better to consider strategic change and leadership change concurrently than to wait and hope that the current leadership eventually develops the skill to reinvent the business.

It is clear that discussions about strategy and succession in a context of change will be very difficult conversations for most family and founder-led busi-nesses. Leaders in place, particularly founders, are not likely to take kindly to questions about their own ability to take the business forward, and potential successors will be loath to bring up the subject, unless it can be couched in impersonal terms of what is good for the business. Again, the starting point has to be a regular, in-depth discussion about strategy; at the same time, the understanding needs to be there that questions of strategy cannot be looked at in isolation from questions about leadership and succession. Like the discus-sion about strategy, the discussion about succession has to be continuous, not necessarily with the idea of making a move right away, but always with the mindset of preparing people and therefore also the business for the next step.

The vast literature on change management is unequivocal about the need to get all the pieces in place. By any measure and even if the analysis that leads to the changes is accurate, poor execution accounts for the majority of failed strategic change projects. In addition to leadership succession, decision makers therefore need to ask themselves if (a) the business has the competences in place to survive and excel in the new environment, and if not, how these competences can be built, and if b) stakeholders within and outside the organization can be counted on to support the changes being proposed. Only if the answers to these questions are satisfactory does succession for change have a realistic chance of working out.

In family and founder-led businesses, perhaps even more so than in publicly listed companies, the ongoing support of key shareholders is critical. A successor for change can only accomplish what is expected of him or her, if shareholders stand behind the strategic transformation in full recognition of the effects it will have on the value of their investment (more or less risky with the new strategy) and the form of their legacy (more or less permanent with the new strategy). Imagine the opposite scenario in which a founder withholds support from his/her successor or a considerable number of family shareholders oppose the intended changes: under these conditions, any successor for change will struggle, spend an inordinate amount of time battling divergent views and may fail. Therefore, it is crucial that important shareholders understand and accept the consequences of succession for change or, alternatively, agree to sell or put their shares in trust.

Succession for change has far-reaching implications for strategy and hence also for organization and ownership. These implications need to be taken into account when considering succession for change. The best way to do so is to recognize and spell out the consequences of the transformation in strategy that will accompany the successful implementation of succession for change. In this way, all stakeholders, and especially family shareholders and founders can gauge the full effect of agreeing to what is far more than just a change of the nameplate on the door of the person at the top.

8.2   Succession and … Power

Even if the impermanence of competitive advantage forces family and founder-led businesses to consider succession in a less episodic manner, it is still going to remain an exceptional event, a once in five years or once in ten years reshuffling of the cards for the business. If succession is for continuity, then many of the characteristics that make the business what it is—the strategy, the organization, the relationship with stakeholders—stay the same, allowing people and structures to continue largely as before. If succession is for change, on the other hand, everything is in play. As a result, the conflict engendered by succession for change goes far beyond personal rivalries: when succession for change is on the table, shareholders and their families, senior managers, even business units and departments are likely to fight to maintain their share of power and influence in the organization. Unless this power struggle is clearly addressed by decision-makers, the process of succession for change can degenerate into a conflict of Shakespearian proportions.

To some degree, the recommendations already made in Chaps. 7 and 8, namely to treat the succession process as continuous and integrate it into the strategy process, mitigate the potential for all out conflict. Thus, if succession for change is part of the regular discourse of decision-makers, it is less likely to be experienced as a shock to the system. Still, there is no getting away from the fact that succession for change will have a significant effect on people and structures, and some conflict is therefore inevitable. The important thing is to channel this conflict in such a way that it does not have a debilitating effect on the business.

The most important thing to do is to take the concerns of people seriously and to include a wide variety of voices in the strategy cum succession process. The wider the variety of voices, the better decision-makers will be able to understand emerging threats and opportunities, giving them more to go on when deciding upon what markets to pursue and what resources to invest in. Including a wide variety of voices also has the salutary effect of generating buy-in for change, as people can see that their input is respected. Now, this kind of broadly based input gathering may already be part of best practice in the strategy process, but it is far less common in the succession process. In contrast to the strategy process, the succession process typically still takes place behind closed doors, with the decision emerging from a Vatican-like cloud of secrecy. Our recommendation is to make the succession for change process more transparent, drawing on inputs from the population of relevant stakeholders and sharing interim progress reports with these same stakeholders.

Going Against the Conventional Wisdom:
The succession process has to take place behind closed doors.—
Closed doors protect the succession process from undue outside influence and allow the people in the business to get on with their work without having to worry about what eventual changes in the power structure will do to their jobs. If the doors to the succession process were open or even just slightly ajar, so the conventional wisdom goes, the process would be subject to manipulation, and the level of uncertainty in the organization would be unbearable. These arguments stand up better in the context of succession for continuity than in the context of succession for change. When continuity is the strategic objective, it is particularly important to keep game playing and uncertainty to a minimum; power should pass from one generation to the next as smoothly as possible, so as not to upset the trajectory of the business. When change is the strategic objective, on the other hand, outside attempts to influence the process and widespread worries about the future are inevitable, no matter how tightly locked the doors.
Succession for change affects a wide range of people, shareholders, executives, and employees. In order to take their reactions into account, their input must be included in the discussions leading to the selection of a new leader. The emphasis here is not on

the person per se, but on making change happen. Opening up the succession process ensures that back door dealing is minimized and employees know where the organization is headed. The idea is not to turn every discussion about succession into a town hall meeting, but rather to enable the proverbial town hall to offer suggestions and voice opinions about what kind of leadership is needed to take the business forward. Based on this input, the people making the decision about succession for change, the current leader and his or her closest advisors, will have a much better grounded idea of what the major stakeholders want and of what the organization needs.

Succession is always a very sensitive topic, for the leadership in place, for potential successors, and for all other stakeholders. Succession for change is even more delicate and raises many more questions. Closed doors on the succession process can distort and even subvert succession for change. Some degree of openness in the succession process is therefore desirable, when strategic change is the objective.

Family and founder-led businesses are by nature more secretive than publicly listed corporations—they do not have to publish quarterly or even annual reports and they do not have to answer to as many outside stakeholders. Although opening up the strategy and especially the succession process to input from stakeholders goes against these businesses' habit of secrecy, in the context of a limited number of key stakeholders, it is actually not that difficult to do. In family and founder-led businesses, there are not so many people to consult with and include in the process. Soliciting the ideas and maintaining the support of major shareholders and senior executives is a way of recognizing that succession for change affects not only the lives of the family leader or the founder, but also the lives of all those around him/her. They, the people who will carry on after the succession, have to understand and accept the thinking behind succession for change. If the process is thus seen as fair, they are more likely to be willing to work with the successor for change and continue to contribute to strategic discussions as the business goes forward. In this sense, the last succession decision creates the good (or bad) basis for the next succession decision.

In changing the existing balance of power, succession for change also affects the corporate governance of the firm. Concretely, a new leader is given a mandate to put in place a new strategy, with potential repercussions for both the scope of individual power and the risk of the business. The new leader may assume much more power than the old (or conversely, if the founder stays on in the role of the Chair, not be allowed sufficient freedom), and the new strategy may take the firm into waters that its risk management systems are not equipped to handle. Much like in the discussion of who is affected by succession for change above, these are developments that can and should be anticipated. Major change of any kind puts a strain on corporate governance, and, as it goes to the heart of power in the corporation, succession for change poses a particular challenge to governance.

Implemented as we advocate, the strategy cum succession process therefore also must include consideration of how succession for change will impact corporate governance. When preparing succession for change and the transformation it entails, decision-makers need to think through how structures of leadership and control can be adapted to the new situation. Specifically, stakeholders may want to put explicit limits on the discretionary powers of leadership (as well as on the discretionary powers of the Chair, if relevant) and upgrade the existing risk management system to make it capable of capturing the potential problems inherent in the new strategy. If there is not yet a board of directors with independent members in place, succession for change may be the right time to think about building or reinforcing such a body. In times of change, corporate governance, too, has to be alive and responsive to the questions raised by the new balance of power in the firm.

8.3   Advice for Advisors

Not all families and not all founder-led businesses will agree to the framework for succession as transformation we have outlined here. Indeed, it may be seen by many as too radical and too invasive, putting too much weight on the process of succession. We can only restate the main argument: in a context of impermanent competitive advantage, succession for change represents an entrepreneurial choice, and succession for continuity often represents the unwillingness to make an entrepreneurial choice. Where a true entrepreneurial choice is being considered, it is not possible to look at succession in isolation from strategy and governance. On the contrary, in family and founder-led businesses, succession offers a highly symbolic and significant opportunity to set a new direction.

Accepting the challenge of succession for change and understanding succession as transformation has a profound effect on the scope of the task of advisors. Not only do they have to master the financial and legal mechanics of succession, they also have to provide guidance on strategy and governance. In our review of the evolution of succession services in Chap. 5, we concluded that the industry was responding to the changing needs of its clients by putting new emphasis on strategic analysis and offering more comprehensive advice. The arguments made in this chapter reinforce the conclusion that succession services are moving in the right direction. Specialist advice still has a place, but only in the context of a broader offering that addresses the need of family and founder-led businesses to rethink what succession is for.

The analysis of the consequences of succession suggests that advisors will need to be more deeply involved in the process of implementing the transformation that succession for change is designed to drive. If succession for change is a process that starts with strategy conversations and ends with adjustments to governance, then succession service providers have to think about how they can accompany their clients over the longer period of time required to see such a transformation through. Not only do advisors need to have a deep understanding of the business they are consulting to and be able to offer a full range of services, from leadership selection to governance, they also have to become experts at change management and be willing to work closely with their clients on implementing succession for change. This means working with many different stakeholders and adjusting to emerging needs over time.

Going Against the Conventional Wisdom:
Succession advisors are primarily concerned with the selection of a leader.—
Succession advice comes in many shapes and sizes and ranges from narrow specifics to comprehensive consulting services. With the exception of finance, tax, and legal specialists, every advisor will provide some kind of input on leader selection: the psychologist will offer advice based on family and top team dynamics, the executive search firm will propose candidates based on job profiles and resumes, and the strategy consultant will make suggestions about leadership based on the needs of the business. In cases where succession is the assignment, the discussion of who is to lead the business may take on so much importance that other concerns are put aside or neglected. Taking succession for change seriously, however, implies that advisors get deeply involved in all aspects of the succession process, not just leadership succession per se, and stay involved over the time necessary to see the desired changes come to fruition. In the ideal case, leadership choice is only the most visible result of a comprehensive analysis that starts with strategy and follows through to governance.

In calling on advisors in questions of succession and strategy, therefore, decision makers at family and founder led businesses need to be willing to open up and look at the big picture. Where succession for change is in the cards, everything has to be fair game, and advisors have to be allowed broad access to all the different stakeholders. There is a very real danger that the succession process thus conceived opens a can of worms: broken relationships among family members and other insiders, broken promises of advancement, and, even, broken business models. Considering succession for change is not for the faint of heart: it challenges both incumbent leaders and advisors to be completely honest with each other about what the business needs.

Advice to family and founder-led businesses: develop long-term relationships with advisors so that they can really get to know your business and all the relevant players, and be prepared to engage them for the long haul—the completion of one succession process leads to the start of the next. Advice to advisors: seek out those family and founder-led businesses that you have the expertise to work with and be ready to engage for the long haul—if the succession process in continuous rather than episodic, it never really comes to an end.

Succession for change does not stop on the day when power is handed over. Not all advisors will be able to offer the kind of process support that family and founder-led businesses need and that we are advocating. In essence, many advisors are still set up to help put in place succession for continuity and are therefore not suited to advising on succession for change. Those firms that decide to focus on succession for change will find a new, growing market, a market in which one size does not fit all and the rules of engagement are not yet cast in stone. With so much at stake for family and founder-led businesses in succession for change, advisors will need to be especially careful about guarding strict neutrality and avoiding being used as unwitting pawns in the struggle for power that is inherent to the exercise. What is good for the business of the client always needs to be the first question on the advisor's mind, especially when stakeholders to a disputed succession are calling. Indeed, succession service providers should develop policies for how to deal with cases in which they risk being set up by one party against another.

8.4   Conclusion

This chapter presented a framework for understanding succession as transformation. The purpose in doing so was to help decision-makers recognize and address the consequences of succession for change in the implementation process. In particular, we singled out the effects of succession for change on the strategy and on the balance of power and explained how an inclusive succession process can reinforce strategic choices and mitigate power struggles. We argued that the succession process needs to go hand in hand with the strategy process and that transparency about the analysis should be the guiding principle in dealing with stakeholders. In line with

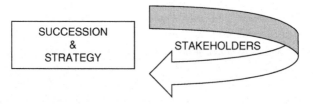

Fig. 8.1 Succession, strategy, and stakeholders

the argument for a more inclusive and less episodic succession process and in light of the significant stakes, we proposed that if they are employed, external advisors (succession service providers) should accompany the succession process from inception to implementation and take special care to maintain strict neutrality throughout.

In the concluding chapter, we turn our attention to succession governance. We want to take a closer look at who makes decisions about succession, how these decisions are made, and what should be the role of the different actors involved, namely the leader, the ownership group, the board of directors, and senior management. Whereas Chaps. 7 and 8 described the processes and consequences of succession for change, Chap. 9 explicitly focuses on the people involved in the succession drama, their motivations and their behaviors (Fig. 8.1).

9

Rethinking Succession Governance

Leader. If the current leader (especially the founder of the business or a family member or non-family executive who has had a great influence on the business), can play a constructive part in the succession process, the probability of a smooth transition is vastly increased.

Ownership. The process of succession should focus the attention of the ownership group and trigger a discussion about the business as an asset. Succession for change should not be a surprise for the ownership group.

Board of Directors. Succession is a process where a board of directors is particularly well placed to add value. Even if it does not have formal responsibility for the succession process, a board of directors can serve as the conscience of the succession process.

Senior Management. Putting key managers in charge of experimenting with new business models gives change efforts a real chance to succeed. Preparing strategic change goes hand in hand with preparing succession for change.

The succession process determines who will be in power, and most treatments of corporate governance therefore devote considerable space to succession. Thus, governance handbooks usually stipulate that a succession process be put in place, that a separate succession committee be constituted (by the board of directors), and that significant shareholders be consulted. More attention is typically paid in corporate governance to the structure of the succession process than to the running of the succession process. In this chapter, we focus on the running of the succession process in the context of succession for change

© The Author(s) 2017
H. Korine, *Succession for Change*, DOI 10.1007/978-3-319-52120-6_9

in family and founder-led businesses. In particular, we describe the roles and responsibilities of the different players involved—current leadership, owner-ship group, board of directors, and senior management—and specify how they should interact over the course of the process.

The role of the current leader (ship) in the succession process in family and founder-led businesses is a subject of considerable debate. On the one hand, advisors often refer to two conventions intended to ensure a fair and objective succession process: one, that the current leader not take part in the process; and, two, that the current leader resign from all roles in the business once the succession process is completed. On the other hand, and although these conventions make sense in the abstract, observers also acknowledge that the idea of exclusion does not reflect the reality of who is in power in family and founder-led businesses. In these settings, a succession process that does not include the current family leader or the founder would be seen as artificial and lacking in legitimacy. Thus, succession governance in family and founder-led businesses first of all requires careful specification of the role of the current leader in the succession process.

In the preceding chapters, we argued that succession for change differs from succession for continuity in the challenges it poses to decision makers. In particular, we noted that succession for change is better addressed as a con-tinuous, not an episodic process and that inclusion and transparency should be preferred to exclusion and secrecy where key stakeholders are concerned. In effect, the succession process becomes part of strategic decision-making in the firm. Re-conceptualizing the succession process in this way also implies rethinking succession governance. In other words, new guidelines need to be established for a succession process that is continuous and inclusive and takes place in the presence of the current leadership.[1]

New rules and safeguards are all the more important as the various groups who need to be involved in the process of succession for change in family and founder-led businesses not only break with convention by drawing on the current leadership, they also include potential successors: the ownership group, the board of directors, and the senior management are all likely to incorporate members of the next generation and/or non-family executives who are candidates for the top job. In practice, every one of the key decision-making groups may be thus mixed, setting the stage for multiple conflicts of interest where succession and strategy are concerned. In this constellation, it is imperative to clearly define roles and responsibilities.

---

[1] An excellent example of how this can work in practice is provided in Glemser AC (2013) "J.M. Huber: A family of solutions", IMD case, IMD-3-2417.

In family and founder-led businesses, corporate governance cannot skirt the particularistic interests of key stakeholders, namely family shareholders and founders, in the name of what is good for the business. Unlike in publicly listed companies and other institutional settings where power bases are more widely dispersed, the key stakeholders in family and founder-led businesses are simply too strong to ignore. Thus, critical decisions, and succession for change is among the most critical in the life of a business, have to be guided by consideration of both the economics of strategy and the politics of particularistic interests. The quality of succession governance should be measured against how well it meets both of these criteria. In the following, we examine the roles and responsibilities of the different groups involved in decision-making about succession and suggest how the succession process can be set up to explicitly address both economics and politics.

9.1   The Leader

The convention of excluding the current leader from the process of choosing his/her own successor derives from the twin goals of preventing entrenchment and preserving objectivity. Entrenchment of an existing power structure is seen as furthering the interests of the few over the many, and any threat to objectivity is seen as potentially endangering the well being of the business. In family and founder-led businesses, the interests of the few, namely of the family and/or of the founder represent the interests of the key stakeholders, and the future of the business does not exist in an interest-free vacuum, but depends on the ongoing support of the key stakeholders. This is why the current leader, whether family or founder, has to be included in the succession process.

The convention of excluding the current leader from all roles in the business once the succession process is completed aims at making sure that the current leader does not continue to run the business from behind the scenes and in effect invalidate the succession. This second convention of exclusion is relevant to family and founder-led businesses and especially pertinent to succession for change, particularly in cases where the current leader did not want to leave office and/or does not support the strategy change advocated by his/her successor. However, because the family or founder will preserve a certain degree of influence no matter what his/her formal role in the business, a blanket rule of exclusion does not make sense. Rather than excluding the current leader, it is better to work with the person to define the scope of his/her role following succession.

Necessarily involved in the succession process, the current leader should work to establish the practices that are required to find the candidate or the candidates that are best suited to take the business forward while taking into account the interests of the key stakeholders. First and foremost, this means that the current leader needs to create or refine existing mechanisms for developing strategy that alert the business to possibilities for change. In succession for change, strategy development and people development go hand in hand and occur continuously, so the current leader will be developing people who are capable of taking the business in a new direction (or in multiple new directions). At the same time, the current leader has to make sure that the interests of key stakeholders (including his/her own interests, of course) find a responsive ear in the strategy cum succession process. As these interests can and do evolve over time, repeated soundings are required. Even if the current leader is not a key stakeholder (i.e. not a member of the owner family), he/she needs to make sure that their interests are made explicit and represented.

By making the process transparent and acknowledging particularistic interests, the current leader can go a long way towards enabling a succession process that is as objective as necessary for the business and realistic for the context. Of course, he/she cannot do this alone, but needs the support of the ownership group and the board of directors, working along the same lines and using the same criteria for making decisions. Rather than asking the current leader to accomplish the psychologically impossible task of removing himself/herself, we are proposing that the current leader take an active role in thinking about the future of the business. The focus should be on moving the business forward under conditions that make sense to the key stakeholders.

If there is a concrete need for the current leader to stay on in some capacity after the succession process is completed, this need has to be spelled out during the process and provided for. Examples include ambassadorial tasks such as maintaining key customer contacts or continuing liaison activities with key stakeholders. This may or may not involve a position on the board. In any case, it is important that the retiring leader buy in to the strategic change the succession aims to accomplish and leave the central role in managing the change to the new leader. Conversely, the new leader, the ownership group, and the board of directors should not accept a role that puts the retiring leader at the center of leading the change his/her successor is supposed to drive.

If the current leader, especially if he/she is the founder of the business or a family member or non-family executive who has had a great influence on the business, can play a constructive part in the succession process, the probability of a smooth transition is vastly increased. This is where the mantle of the leader effect discussed in Chap. 1 can come to bear on the successor.

Table 9.1 Leadership involvement in the succession process: do's & don'ts

	Do	Don't
Set up	Establish guidelines	Exclude any options
Stakeholder MGMT	Sound out and inform	Force acceptance of terms
Candidate selection	Review and recommend	Insist on personal criteria
Post succession	Seek out a fitting role	Shadow lead change

Conversely, if the current leader is very influential, but for the personal and psychological reasons described in Chap. 1 cannot let go, then it is better to limit the leader's involvement and rely more heavily on the ownership group (to the extent that it is independent of the leader) and the board of directors. Following this line of reasoning, Table 9.1 summarizes the desired types of involvement of the current leader in the succession process in terms of do's and don'ts.

9.2 The Ownership Group

A founder may be the leader and the sole owner of a business, with only himself/herself to consult on questions of ownership. In family businesses of any size and of any longevity, however, it is highly likely that there will be an ownership group that includes additional people, both members active in the business and members who are only connected to the business via their shareholdings. Ideally, the ownership group is organized in a separate structure, with its own rules for when and how to interact with the business.[2] Where succession for change is the objective, the ownership group needs to play a role in the succession process that goes beyond just being informed; it has to make its voice heard in the process.

Succession can affirm strategic continuity or it can herald strategic change; either way, the process of succession should focus the attention of the ownership group and trigger a discussion about the business as an asset. What does the ownership group want to do with the asset? Are they still the right owners for the asset going forward? Succession for continuity implies that the major variables of interest to the ownership group—dividend policy, investment risk, and stakeholder relationships—will not be substantially affected. Succession for change, on the other hand, will affect these variables, either in

---

[2] The well-known three-circle model developed by Renato Tagiuri and John A. Davis provides the logic for constituting a separate ownership structure. See "Bivalent Attributes of the Family Firm." (1982) Working paper, Harvard Business School, Cambridge, MA. Reprinted (1996) in Family Business Review, Vol. IX, No. 2, pp. 199–208.

a positive or a negative direction. Thus, a succession that is aimed at boosting international growth, for example, will most likely imply a reduced dividend, a temporarily (at least) increased investment risk, and more difficult relationships with local stakeholders. A succession aimed at selling a part of the business and refocusing on core competences, on the other hand, will have the opposite effects, at least in the short term. The ownership group needs to be clear on what it wants for the business, and planning for succession gives it the occasion to revisit this question.

Going Against the Conventional Wisdom:
The ownership group should not get involved in the succession process.—
Particularly in larger family businesses that span multiple generations of ownership, it has become common practice to follow the publicly listed company mantra of separating ownership and control. In other words, owners own, and managers manage; the role of ownership is often conceived of as passive, and the role of management is often delegated to non-owner managers. Some authors even refer to the latter as "professional managers", to distinguish them from supposedly unprofessional family involvement in the business. In businesses such as these, ownership interest and ownership competence tend to wane over time. As a result, key decisions about strategy and succession are first debated among non-family managers and directors before being submitted to the ownership group for ratification. In some cases, particularly where succession is for continuity and the ownership group is happy to let others decide for them, this works out fine. However, where succession is for change, and one cannot count on a passive ownership group, this modus operandi is fraught with danger, for both managers and owners.

Succession for change directly affects the quality of the ownership group's asset, changing both its risk profile and its time horizon. For this reason, structures need to be put in place to allow the ownership group to internally discuss and then communicate its interest in the succession process. One cannot assume that the ownership group will agree to precooked decisions by rubber stamp. The ownership group may be internally split; previously passive individuals may not be willing to stay quiet any longer; and, even where the ownership group does not have the business competence to discuss succession, some members may want to have their say. Much better than risking opposition down the line, therefore, to include the ownership group in succession discussions from early on.

In view of the important position of the ownership group in key decisions such as succession, it is important to work with them on a continuous basis, to keep them involved in the governance of the business. Strict separation of ownership and control does not make sense in family and founder-led businesses, particularly where governance questions are concerned. Lack of consultation, on the part of management, and lack of interest and competence, on the part of ownership may be the current reality, but this is not a stable equilibrium. At the latest when succession for change is on the table, management and ownership will have to work together.

In an ownership group of any size, it is clear that not all shareholders will necessarily agree on the same strategy for the business. Typically, there will be a divide between those willing to support investment for growth and those wishing to focus on maintaining or even increasing dividends. In the event of significant disagreement, a shareholder agreement that specifies rules for buying and selling provides a "neutral" point of reference and can prevent deadlocks. The ultimate outcome of the confrontation of opposing interests has to feed into the succession process. How this is done in practice depends on the structures in place for communicating the view of the ownership group which in turn are typically determined by the size and the age of the business: shareholder resolution, representation in the board of directors, or direct input to the acting leadership.

Because members of the ownership group may also be personally affected by the succession decision in terms of their career in the business, it is important that the ownership group come to a decision that is backed up by a careful consideration of the issues and properly documented. Members of the next generation deserve particular consideration, even if they are not formally part of the ownership group. After all, succession for change affects not only their eventual stakes in the business but also their future chances for succession. Depending on where succession for change takes the business, there may or may not be a place for them. Again, the watchwords in family and founder-led businesses considering succession for change should be continuous process involvement and inclusion. Succession for change cannot be a surprise for the ownership group.

9.3   The Board of Directors

In publicly listed firms as well as in many other kinds of institutions, ultimate responsibility for succession rests with the board of directors. Comprised of senior personalities, many of whom are preferably independent of both ownership and current management, the board of directors is supposed to make its choice on the basis of what is best for the firm or the business. In family and founder-led businesses, the role and place of the board of directors is not as clear. Many of the firms that fall under these two categories do not even have a board of directors, and of those who do, only a few (typically the largest) will give much weight to independent directors. The reality of most family and founder-led businesses that are not publicly listed is that a board of directors is nice to have, but is not seen as essential to the ongoing success of the business.

Although this book is not the place to try to convince family and founder-led businesses of the general value of a strong and at least to some degree independent board of directors, we do wish to point out that succession is a process in which a board of directors is particularly well placed to add value. This is because many of the questions around the different interests of the various stakeholders—shareholders who disagree among themselves, managers who are vying for position, and members of the next generation who are building their careers—crystallize during succession. Even if it is not neutral, in the sense of being led by independent directors, a board with independent directors offers an alternative forum for bringing the different interests around succession into the open. Where succession is for change, these differences are likely to be particularly severe, and a forum for airing these differences that includes at least a few respected outsiders is especially important.

Going Against the Conventional Wisdom:
    The board of directors has to have control over the succession process.—
    A board of directors and independent board members do not in and of themselves represent a magic cure for all the governance ills that may beset a firm. More than twenty years of board-focused governance reform in publicly listed companies have gone to show that there is only so much a board can do. For this reason, family and founder-led businesses should be as wary of the "board solution" as they are of other governance recipes passed on from the arena of publicly listed companies. Any solution has to fit the particular context. That being said, a board of directors, properly constituted, can add value, especially in a process of succession for change. How—by bringing in different perspectives on competition that family and founder might not be aware of; by sharing its experience from other succession situations; and, perhaps most importantly, by providing a safe forum for airing the interests and concerns of all stakeholders.
    In family and founder-led businesses, the board of directors is unlikely to meet strict definitions of independence. Typically, and this is generally by choice, not by necessity, board members will have some previous tie to the business and/or to its major stakeholders. The advantage of having this kind of tie is that board members know and care deeply about the business; decision-makers in turn put their trust board members that they have known a long time. Unless a board member is completely taken in by one stakeholder (the "friend of Bill" syndrome) or dependent upon his or her position on the board, these are very good prerequisites for productive involvement in strategy and succession decisions. Not formally independent, but intellectually independent and personally committed to the good of the business, these are the best kind of board members for family and founder-led businesses.
    In good times and when no major decisions are in the offing, many family and founder-led businesses can dispense with a board of directors, if they are not legally required to have one. It is when the course of the business needs to be set or reset that

a board can be very useful, if not essential in offering perspective and maintaining trust. The problem is that such a board cannot be made to appear out of thin air, but needs to be built up over time. Thus, even smaller family and founder-led businesses may find that a well running board is a worthwhile investment.

The influence of the family and/or the founder may be strong, but respected outsiders on a board of directors can still play an important role in helping to manage or even guiding the succession process. Thus, they can be accessible to all parties and may on occasion meet in private (i.e. without the current family leader or founder) to discuss questions of a sensitive or personal nature. Most importantly, respected outsiders on a board of directors can ensure that the focus of the succession process always stays on the strategy and the future of the business and does not get hijacked by the current leadership or disintegrate into a free for all of different interests. Even if it does not have formal ownership of the succession process, a board of directors can and should serve as the conscience of the succession process. Before becoming members and while they are on the board, independent directors should ask themselves if they are willing and able to fulfill that critical function.

9.4 Senior Management

Senior management and any members of the next generation that belong to senior management also play critical roles in the succession process. As candidates for succession, they are interested actors in the process; as providers of input on the state of the business, they are contributors who help shape the process. Decision-makers, principally the current leadership, the ownership group, and the board of directors, need to make sure that senior management have the chance to fulfill both of these roles to the best of their abilities. This means that decision-makers have to give members of the senior management opportunities to show if they are capable of leading change and have to find a way to take the input of senior management on board in mulling over what strategic changes to make.

Not all senior managers need to be considered for the top job. Some do not have the ability, and others do not have the perspective, in terms of age or experience. When succession for change is the objective, those that do merit consideration have to be encouraged to try their hand at the new business models that may take the firm into the future, without the fear of being penalized if the business model they are testing does not work out. This does not mean that candidates for succession to the top job should be allowed to experiment endlessly or be confined to the new business model track. Instead, valid candidates should be tested on their ability to run both existing core businesses and new business models. This takes time, but in a succession process that is geared towards driving change, the time of business and personal development is part of the succession process.

Going Against the Conventional Wisdom:

Candidates for succession should not run businesses outside the core.—

One of the raps against insiders in succession is that they do not have sufficient experience in developing and running businesses outside the core. As long as the core is healthy and can be expected to continue doing well for the foreseeable future, strategic change is not an issue and insiders do not need to build experience outside the core. Change of the kind we have seen over the last twenty-five years makes this happy state of affairs increasingly unlikely, even for the most dominant businesses, and puts insiders at a severe disadvantage when succession for change is being considered. In many cases of succession for change, family and founder-led businesses have not provided senior managers with meaningful experience outside the core and therefore have to turn to outsiders for new leadership, with all the integration and acceptance challenges that implies.

By leading change from the ground up senior managers who are legitimate candidates for succession can prepare themselves for the top job and contribute in a meaningful way to the strategic dialogue that shapes the future of the firm, as it evolves into new business areas. Again, for strategic reasons as well for leadership development reasons, new, outside businesses need to be connected to the core in some way. This connection is what makes sure that the exotic flowers will be watered and their managers valued in the larger organization. It is too easy to say that, for their own protection, new businesses need to be kept at a distance from the core. Better to nurture them and their leaders under realistic conditions of interdependence with the core, in full knowledge of the difficulty of doing so.

Putting key managers in charge of experimenting with new business models gives change efforts a real chance to succeed. It provides the basis for informing decision makers about new markets and new resources in a way that mere exploratory studies or consulting reports cannot. In effect, senior managers can build the necessary bridges between old and new businesses, preparing both the organization and decision makers for change. For this to happen, it is critical that senior managers, both those working on new business models and those working on existing core businesses, be made a part of the broader process of strategic thinking at the highest levels.

Preparing strategic change goes hand in hand with preparing succession for change. It is clear that senior managers who are candidates for succession can never be disinterested parties in the process of succession for change. In our view, they should be key contributors to the process.

9.5 Conclusion

This chapter outlined a framework for thinking about the governance of the succession process. When succession for change is the objective, the emphasis of succession governance shifts from executive selection to strategic direction. All of the actors involved in the succession process in family and founder-led businesses, the leader, the ownership group, the board of directors, and the senior management, need to understand and act upon succession in terms of the business. Of course, personal preferences, interpersonal allegiances, and stakeholder interests all play a role in the succession process, even more so in the case of succession for change than in the case of succession for continuity. By defining the roles and responsibilities of the various actors in a realistic manner and emphasizing the needs of the business, succession governance that is strategically focused provides a means of addressing the conflicts of interest that inevitably accompany succession.

One of the truisms in the field is that even successful family businesses only rarely survive past the third generation. Traditionally, this broadly supported empirical finding is explained by dysfunctions in the family and the failure to adequately prepare for leadership succession. When, as in the economic environment of the last twenty-five years, businesses need to evolve very quickly and succession for change becomes imperative, we can expect the lives of family businesses to shorten. More family and founder-led

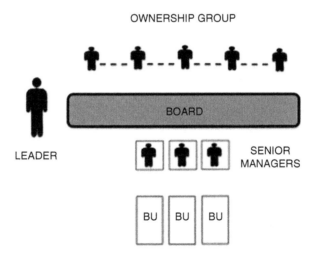

Fig. 9.1 Roles in succession governance

businesses will sell out and more will fail to negotiate the strategic transitions required to stay alive in a context of more dynamic competition. A framework for succession governance that speaks directly to the questions raised in preparing for succession for change should help some family and founder-led businesses continue to reach and maybe even surpass the hurdle of the third generation (Fig. 9.1).

Epilogue. Succession—The Most Human of Governance Challenges

When Christian Pitschen-Melchior spent seven years hand drilling a viewing gallery into the rocks overlooking the spectacular Rofflafall waterfalls in the mountains of eastern Switzerland, he was creating a unique but nonetheless archetypical family business, one that has continued to exist essentially unchanged for well over one hundred years now: a basis in fixed assets, a distinct competitive position, a steady income for the family and a legacy of devotion to the site. Like the waterfalls it is named after, Rofflafall is built for the ages, and Pitschen-Melchior's fifth generation successors carry on just as the founder intended, when a visit to the Niagara Falls inspired him to abort the immigration process and create his own version of the North American tourist attraction in the cliffs over the Rhine above his grandparents' inn. In a business built for the sole purpose of making it possible for tourists to experience a spectacle accessible only via a viewing gallery hewn into stone, succession has to be for continuity. Until they sell, if indeed a buyer could ever be found, the descendants of Pitschen-Melchior remain tied to Rofflafall and the original conception of the business.

In a sense, the Melchior family has it easy—there is no strategic choice to be made. Not every family or founder-led business is as rigidly tied to the original strategy. Fixed assets may be used for different purposes or sold; the competitive position may be altered, the income may be reinvested in new businesses, and the legacy may be revised. As we have seen, however, change is difficult and continuity remains the norm in family and founder-led businesses. Even though they could, and in many cases indeed should take steps to redirect the business, the leaders of family and founder-led businesses generally prefer succession for continuity. The legacy effect makes them treat the business and its policies and norms as if they were hewn into stone.

© The Author(s) 2017
H. Korine, *Succession for Change*, DOI 10.1007/978-3-319-52120-6

Succession is first and foremost a human drama that mirrors the passing of generations—from parents to children. In family and founder-led businesses, the personification of leadership accentuates the mythological aspects of succession. The shaper of a joint destiny moves on, and the orphaned organization remains to fend for itself. In other words, succession touches the very essence of what it means to be human: growing older and letting go. Against this background, it is only fitting that succession has drawn a lot of attention from students of the human psyche. Succession is human, but as it is about who is in power, it is also fundamentally political. However personal, succession implies a struggle among individuals over the right to step into the shoes of the current leader and take the organization forward. Even where succession is for continuity, rivalry and conflict are likely. In the case of succession for change, confrontation of different interests is inevitable.

So human and so political, succession for change has always provided fascinating data for historians and excellent raw material for dramatists. The successions that make the best stories center on personal ambition, hinge on dramatic episodes, and involve small circles of conspirators. Shakespeare's unparalleled ability to capture the drama of succession ensures that King Lear, Macbeth, and Hamlet are alive and well in the consciousness of decision-makers the world over. These were all cases of succession for change that went terribly wrong. In this book, we have tried to show how succession for change can, on the contrary, be made to work out for the good of the organization. To do so, we have had to define a new approach to the human and political challenges raised by succession for change.

Where classical treatments of succession for change in literature focus on personal ambition, dramatic episodes, and small circles of conspirators (decision-makers), we have emphasized strategic objectives, continuous processes, and inclusive decision-making. Where the traditional approach is based on capturing power over the organization by force, our approach is based on winning power over the organization by persuasion. This is not to say that personal ambition, drama, and conspiracy go away in today's family and founder-led businesses. Nor do we underestimate the practical difficulty of transforming the succession process according to our framework. And yet, if competitive advantage is short-lived and succession must be for change, then we cannot accept Shakespearean drama and failure as the norm. Much as business itself, the way we think about succession needs to evolve.

Succession is still human and political, and succession for change even more so, but we can now offer an alternative pathway to resolving an age-old question.

Index[1]

A
Apple, 28–30, 42, 43, 45
automobile industry, 28, 31, 34

B
biotechnology, 27, 30–2
board of directors, 20, 44, 100,
    103, 105, 106, 108, 109,
    111–13, 115
Buffett, 83

C
capital intensity, 33
competitive advantage, x, 27–33,
    35, 36, 38, 67, 71,
    77–80, 82, 87–90,
    95, 97, 100, 118
consultant, family business, 51, 53, 55,
    56, 60
consultant, strategy, 51, 55, 57, 58,
    60, 101

D
Dell, 31, 38
Disney, 45, 45n10, 47

E
entrepreneurial choice, x, 37, 94, 95, 100
entrepreneurial values, x, 77, 79, 86,
    86n4, 88, 90
executive selection, x, 115

F
family, ix, x, 3, 15n1, 27–37, 51, 63,
    77, 93, 105–6
family office, 51, 53, 55–8, 83
Ford, 34, 38
founder, x, 3, 17, 27–37, 63, 77,
    93, 105

G
Generation me, 64n1, 67

---

[1] Note: Page numbers followed by "n" denote notes.

© The Author(s) 2017
H. Korine, *Succession for Change*, DOI 10.1007/978-3-319-52120-6

governance, ix, x, 5–7, 9, 16, 16n3, 17, 23, 39, 44, 52, 55, 67, 70, 72, 91, 93, 94, 99–101, 103, 105–18

I

information and communications technology (ICT), 27, 29–34
Infosys, 38
insider(s), 8, 20, 37, 39, 45–9, 50, 77, 82, 101, 114

K

Kering, 49
King David, ix, 9, 9n4, 10–13, 18, 24
King Lear, ix, 10–12, 18, 24, 118

L

leader, role of, 103, 106
leader, tenure, 80, 82
legacy, x, 3–13, 16, 20–2, 24, 70, 78–80, 84, 86, 97, 117
Li Ning, 38
Luxottica, 38

M

Mars, 83–5
Microsoft, 30, 31, 47

N

networks of families, 63, 69–71
next generation, x, xi, 4, 8, 33, 41, 42, 47, 48, 50, 52–5, 59, 63–73, 78, 83, 89, 90, 106, 111–13

O

outsider(s), 8, 23, 37–9, 45–7, 50, 55, 77, 112–14
ownership, role of, 110

P

Pictet, 52n2, 81–4, 88
power, x, 3, 7–11, 13, 20, 42, 43, 45, 90, 93, 94, 97–100, 102, 105–7, 118
psychology, 3, 6–13, 15–18, 24, 56, 59, 64

R

return of family/founder, 37, 42–4
Rofflafall, 117

S

sale(s), 23, 30, 37–42, 46, 50, 58n5, 94
senior management, 103, 105, 106, 113–15
strategy, vi, x, 5, 7, 17, 20, 23, 32, 35, 37, 44, 49, 58–60, 79, 80, 82, 83, 87, 91, 93–102, 106–8, 110–13, 117
succession, best practice, 15, 16, 19–22, 24, 63, 68, 98
succession for change, x, 7, 9–13, 19, 22, 24, 27, 28, 35, 37–51, 55, 59–61, 63, 64, 70–3, 78–80, 83, 86–8, 90, 91, 93–103, 105–16, 118
succession for continuity, x, 4, 7–13, 19, 51, 55, 57, 59, 61, 63, 65, 77, 78, 90, 93, 98, 100, 102, 106, 109, 115, 117
succession in history, 6–8, 11, 12, 51, 54–9, 80
succession in religion, 11
succession planning, 15–19, 22, 24, 52, 56, 60n6, 91
succession process, continuous, 81, 82
succession process, episodic, x, 79, 80, 82–4, 88, 90, 91, 97
succession services, ix, 15, 22–4, 50–61, 68, 77, 100

T

timing of succession, 37, 41, 79, 80, 87, 90, 95

transformation, x, 16, 27–9, 38, 45, 46, 49, 54, 55, 90, 91, 93–103

trusts, 51, 55, 56

V

values, x, 5, 6, 77, 79, 81, 84–8, 90

W

wealth management, 51, 53, 55–7, 58n5

Printed by Printforce, the Netherlands